The Power of Retention:

More Customer Service for Higher Education

Neal A. Raisman, PhD

Published by The Administrators' Bookshelf

86 N Cassady Avenue . Columbus OH 43209
www.adminbookshelf.com

ISBN 978-1-935066-02-6

CONTENTS

About the Author 8

WHY THIS BOOK? 9

The Butterfly Effect 9

Overview 11

RETAINING VERSUS OBTAINING 16

It is Better to Retain than Obtain 16

The Way to Do That – Customer Service 20

The 72% Factor 23

Customer service? For academia? 26

The Rules of Working Here 28

The Customer is... ? 31

WHAT IS CUSTOMER SERVICE IN COLLEGE? 34

Wrong by Their Very Nature as Students 34

Clients. Not customers 36

Pogo is Right Again 41

Durgin Park 45

Hi I'm Don. I'll Be Your Insulter Tonight 48

McService.....50

Serve Customers When They Are Hungry.....53

THE FISCAL POWER OF RETENTION.....57

The Investment to Expectations Relationship.....57

The Difficulty to Pay to Expectation Ratio.....60

A Price More Precious than Rubies.....62

The Fiscal Power of Retention.....64

The Hierarchy of Student Decision-Making.....67

Hierarchy Step 1: Can I Get In?.....70

Hierarchy Step 2: Can I Afford It?.....72

Making Financial Aid Even More Difficult.....75

Ways to Make It Affordable.....78

Hierarchy Step 3: Can I Graduate?.....79

Graduation Is the Goal.....80

LEARN AND EARN.....83

Focus on Helping Them Succeed.....86

Customer Service-Based Scheduling.....88

Figuring the Real Cost of Sections.....90

Cancelling Retention.....93

Hierarchy Step 4: Can I Get a Job?.....95

The Job-Orientation of Students.....96

College – AAA League for Jobs?.....99

We Were Our Students 103

Hierarchy Step 5: Will I Like It? 105

Satisfaction Is Not Enough and Never the Goal 107

Let Them Eat Football 109

Those Who Can Engage – Do 113

Why Students Leave a College 115

CSFS: CUSTOMER SERVICE FACTORS 120

CSFactor 1: The Cost of Attrition 121

CSF2: Figuring Real Admissions and Attrition Costs 124

CSF2: FGE's and Admission Costs 125

CSF 2: Using The Formula 128

CFS3: A Cost or A Bonus 130

Checking Your School's Health 133

RETURN ON INVESTMENT (ROI) 136

Learn and Earn; Not Churn and Burn 136

The Three ROI's 139

Learn and Earn 143

Implementing Learn and Earn 147

Surveys and How to Use Them 149

Metaphoric Surveying 152

Interviewing 156

Don't Believe Tink! 158

Required Attendance is Good Service 164

Customer Service and Fund Raising 168

HAPPIER STUDENTS AND FACULTY 170

Attitude Comes to College 170

Overcoming the Communication Clash 176

Happier Teachers = More Learning 179

Greater Classroom and Teaching Fulfillment/Pleasure 183

Easy Grades are Not Customer Service 185

Service Equity and Faculty Classroom Pleasure at Cheers University 187

Know Their Names 187

Be Glad They Came 189

Leaders Need to Be Customer Service Advocates 191

THE CAMPUS 194

Enrollment, Metaphors and Poetry 194

Campuses Are Not Retreats 197

Losing Enrollment in Lot C 199

Increase the Feeling and Reality of Security on Campus 206

Safety as a Metaphor 206

Ten Quick Security Steps to Increase Safety on Campus 209

Signs of Rites and Wrongs de Passages 212

Interior Signs Can Lead to the Exits 217

A College That Did It Well and Inexpensively 220

HOW TO'S 2255

Good Morning Captain.. 2255

Gordon Gee and the Tie That Binds.. 22929

Get Out of Your Office.. 2311

Make Every Day a Captain K or Bill Schaar Day............................... 2333

Students Hate Lines.. 2355

Techno-Eco Extremism – Cut Down All Phone Trees...................... 2388

Give a Name – Get a Name.. 2422

A Simple Solution to Phone Rudeness... 2466

Three Last Minute Solutions to Retain Students................................ 2488

Greatest Gift of All – Saving Student Enrollment.............................. 2511

Make Them Complain to Improve Customer Service.......................... 2533

THE 15 PRINCIPLES OF GOOD *ACADEMIC* CUSTOMER SERVICE 2577

SOME CONCLUDING THOUGHTS.................................... 2611

About the Author

Dr. Neal A Raisman is the internationally recognized expert on academic customer service and how it affects enrollment, retention and morale of students and college communities. In fact, Raisman is regarded as the founder of the research area and service concerns we know as academic customer service with his 2002 bestselling book Embrace the Oxymoron: Customer Service in Higher Education (LRP Publications). His more than 200 articles and four books are also widely read and regarded.

He founded AcademicMAPS, the leading provider of retention and enrollment solutions through customer service in 1999. The consulting firm has assisted over 200 career schools, colleges, universities as well as businesses and corporations in the US, Europe and Canada with customer service audits, training, workshops, presentations and research.

His blog (www.academicmaps.blogspot.com) is the leading online resources for academic customer service, retention, enrollment and marketing. It's over 100 articles are read by over 36,000 visitors to the site a month.

Dr. Raisman has also held senior administrative positions in doctoral, baccalaureate and community colleges where he has been a chancellor, president, associate provost, dean and faculty member. His academic experience was tempered and subsequent writing was seriously affected by his work as a professional comedian and comedy writer. Though he can speak and write in *academic-ese,* he prefers to write as if people might actually want to read, learn and enjoy his articles and books. In this volume for instance, he writes as if in conversation with the reader. Raisman believes that the messages are best presented as if the reader and author were sitting down over a cup of coffee and not in a formal environment like a classroom or some formal academic journal.

Cover Design by Christopher Sanna

Christopher Sanna designed the cover for this book. He is the nationally renowned graphic designer whose work has been recognized by his peers and clients as creating "brilliantly beautiful and effective pieces of art and commercial art." We are very pleased to have Chris and his firm SANNA (www.sanna.com) as our cover designer.

Why this Book?

The Butterfly Effect

For those of us who went into education with the hope of changing the world and the lives of people for the better, customer service can be a major factor in meeting that mission. It can create what I see as the *butterfly effect* of enrolling, retaining and graduating more students.

The butterfly effect suggests that the simple, slight flapping of delicate butterfly wings can change the course of history. The wings will create an almost unnoticeable but actual change in the air that can have effects on the condition of the atmosphere which in turn can lead to a series of events that could then lead to major change in weather like the creation of a tornado. So from simple, almost imperceptible actions, events, deeds or words, lives can change.

While consulting at Beckfield College in Florence KY, a most perfect example of this theory occurred. Beckfield is a four-year career college with five programs. It has a culture of believing in its students. The staff and faculty really provide levels of personal service that are outstanding.

A mother came to the College to meet with an admission's representative. She brought her daughter with her because she could not get, or maybe afford, a babysitter. The mother and daughter sat with the representative and talked about the Beckfield program and how it could change her life. The representative spent all the time the mother wanted and very personably and carefully explained the program, financial aid and how she believed the mother could succeed. Every question was answered fully and with compassion. The mother it seemed to need a major change in her life but was somewhat unsure of herself. She would be the first in her family to go to college.

She met other people at Beckfield who all took the time to help her and respond to any concerns from paying for school to what to do if she needed extra help having been out of school for quite a while. By the time she had finished meeting with the admission's representative, she had her answers and believed in herself again. She thanked the rep, completed an application, and she and her daughter who had been sitting patiently and hearing everything, started to leave the building.

As they got to the end of the hall, the little girl turned around and ran back toward the admission's rep's office. She ran into the office and stopped. She then reached into her hair where she took out a barrette and handed it to the admission's rep. A small token but one with a huge message within it.

The butterfly effect! The admission's rep had created what some might see as a small change in the air but it was a major shift for the world. Yes, the mother will likely attend Beckfield and she will probably graduate. Her daughter will also see college as a good place, somewhere she will go and Beckfield by the way will have first consideration, I believe.

The mother's family will change for the better. If she goes into nursing, other families will also be changed and helped. The daughter will likely attend college. Her family will be better for it. And her children will benefit and then see college as part of their lives too and so on. The good will spread geometrically and perhaps affect the future of the world itself. Maybe it could seem in small ways, but as the mother and daughter touch others and they touch others and they… Well, you see the progression.

Oh by the way, the barrette the daughter gave the admission's rep. It was a little butterfly.

Overview

Customer service is an overlooked aspect in a school's success. Unfortunately, too many schools have a problem accepting that. They give in to notions that customer service is some business concept that has no or little relevance to a college. People in colleges and universities, especially faculty, have a sense that when anyone discusses customer service in academia it is just a disguised call to pander to students, to lower standards, give the students high grades for little work to make and keep them happy. That is not customer service. That is cheating the client.

Colleges and universities are businesses at their core. Granted, unique and idiosyncratic businesses, but service providers all the same. Each and every one of them has its own culture, mores, folkways, traditions, codes – both written and unwritten – and a language called *academic-ese* that generate its uniqueness. Yet, common to everyone is a business model including budgets, salaries, benefits, personnel, administrations, strategic plans, marketing, customer acquisition, and so on, which make institutes of higher education businesses. And colleges, universities and career colleges all have clients/customers called students and employees that demand services.

Higher education and its more than 4000 individual colleges, universities and career colleges are distinctive from other business models and so customer service needs to recognize that. This is true whether or not the school is a not-for-profit college, a private university or a publicly supported two or four-year college or a for-profit institution. Though some might think that a proprietary school would be significantly different from a not-for-profit, sometimes the only thing separating their basic operational models is that a not-for-profit college calls extra money at the end of the year a fund balance or surplus while the career college calls it profit. They all must deliver a concept called education to customers called students through product parts called courses and majors that are supposed to lead to a finished product that is certified at graduation that is supposed to lead to a job or career. If they don't, they lose their market and the revenue needed to operate.

They are significantly different than other businesses since the final product they create (learning and individual intellectual, professional or technological growth) are both invisible and intangible. Cannot hold an education. Nor smell it. Taste it. Feel it. See it. At best, a graduate and an employer or graduate school may intuit it. Or they must accept the transcript as some evidence that a course of study has been completed at an indicated level of success. Rather unlike the product of a manufacturer, the tangible stock of a store, its products or even the services provided by say a Disneyland. For the education sector, the approaches of the world of retail, commerce, hospitality and corporations do not always work. At best, they need to be adapted to recognize that the services in a school are not exactly equal to selling widgets or serving a meal. Platitudes will not work either. And unlike most every other business or professional service, colleges have to provide services every single day, every single class. Students make a buying decision prior to every class they take. "Should I go to class today? Do I want to go to math today? Do I wish to *buy* Prof. X today?"

It's not like going into a store and purchasing a retail item, taking it to the cashier, getting a smile, a receipt and "Have a nice day." A retail service experience is a one-time moment focused on a particular purchase that lasts maybe five to ten minutes depending on the length of the line. It is repeated only when the customer needs or decides to buy another shirt for example.

In higher education, the experience is a constant, two to six year process in which every day, every class, every encounter with the school from parking to walking to taking classes and meeting with employees becomes a buying or return opportunity for a college's customer.

As a result, the concepts of business, corporations and even hospitality companies do not always apply to higher education. What will work is recognition of concepts such as Learn and Earn and using it to assure that students get the returns on investment they seek. Moreover, the employees at a store, for example, are rather less independent than employees at a college. In a store or restaurant, the management can tell employees, "This is the way we will address customers on the floor. You will say the following when encountering a customer." Just try that with a faculty member for instance, and you will likely not forget the response. Faculty and other university personnel see the campus as different, detached from business and commercial concerns. If one wants to engage them in a discussion or processes of customer retention through appropriate service, that engagement must recognize their needs, attitude and general disdain for a commercial concept such as customer service.

Keep in mind that faculty are not like waiters at a restaurant. Waiters or waitresses just serve what the customer orders and what was prepared for them to bring out of the kitchen. In most every college or university, faculty members are the restaurant owner, executive chefs, maitre de, and floor manager of the eatery called *my class and section.* They own it, staff it and make decisions about it. In their restaurant they are, speaking quite metaphorically, *the soup Nazis* who decide who will get soup and who will be ejected. Administrators might be the landlords but they cannot dictate the menu, serving style or what goes into each course of the meal called an education.

Administrators, trustees and schools must also keep in mind what restaurants must always be concerned with. The core service is itself the final product – the food. A conscientious and considerate waiter can never make up for bad food. But an attentive and pleasant waiter can make good food taste even better and keep customers loyal.

In a school, the product is the education itself. A good education with good customer service will make for greater retention, happier students, and satisfied graduates who will support the school by becoming advocates for it. Perhaps even donating alumni.

And that's what this book is about. How schools can improve their services to their core clients – students and the college community. The methods are not very difficult to implement, nor are they counter-intuitive corporate concepts. They are ones learned from many years of research on college campuses studying how we act and interact. The material and reporting also derives from understanding and listening to our student clients and adapting applicable and successful customer service methods from sources external to academia such as sociology, neuron and cognitive studies, behavioral psychology and what Paco Underhill dubbed *the science of shopping* in his important book *Why We Buy: The Science of Shopping* (1999) to our unique world of academia. These methods have been worked out on many campuses all over the country and in Europe where I have had the privilege to consult, speak, teach and train. They are also quite practical, inexpensive and acceptable to the college community. Generally the processes and techniques costs much less than a student or two and repay the school in many more retained students.

The book will discuss providing quality learning in an appropriate environment that speaks to actual students and offers them opportunities to enjoy themselves and their learning. The book will discuss methods and techniques to make students want to learn more and wish stay at the school. For example, the discussion will focus on helping the students keep focused on their goals in life and career and how the school will help them get to them.

How to do it? Through concepts that focus on retention rather than admissions as a core element of an institution's success. That can help improve your customer service focus.

Understanding what customer service is for an academic environment, implementing it at your school and using the principles of Good Academic customer service is guaranteed to help a school increase its population. For instance, Principle 1 in my list of Fifteen Principles of Good Customer Service for Colleges

:

Every student wants to attend Cheers University
and every employee wants to work there
"...where everybody knows your name
and they're awfully glad you came..."

Sounds easy. And it can be with some simple customer service training that focuses on the business we are in – schools and colleges.

One quick thought to keep in mind when the phrase *customer* is used in this book. It is core to the discussion that it is realized that students are not exactly customers, they are more like clients. A client hires someone to study the situation, indicate what is wrong, and then offer the tools to fix what is needed to succeed. Like clients, students come to the experts (school) to find out what they must do to improve and grow so their futures will be successful. Schools need to understand their student clients, understand what they really need and want, then provide them the academic and social services to strengthen and grow. And though some skeptics might believe it is easy grades with little work that students want, it really is not.

What I have found in my studies of and for schools is that most students want three things. And it all has to do with returns on investment (ROI), particularly three ROI's that relate to the customer in the academic environment. They want to feel an *f-roi,* a solid *e-roi,* a full sense of an *a-roi.* And the book will help you understand and increase your and your students' ROI.

Though this book focuses primarily on students, most everything said for them can be applied to most everyone else in our campus community – even ourselves. We are all customers of one another after all.

Retaining Versus Obtaining

It is Better to Retain than Obtain

I have been told by many a successful administrator that it is easier to sit on top of a flagpole than it is to climb it. Sounds logical. The effort needed to climb up the pole would surely have to require more exertion than finding the balancing point on top of it. Of course, not getting the sitting process or position right could have its problems as well. That gravity stuff can be pesky after all.

In the analogy working here, climbing the pole equates to the recruiting, admitting and enrolling process. It is hard work, time consuming and costs more money that you may realize. Sitting on the pole? That's retention. Holding on to the students you already have. It should be easier to retain students than to obtain them. Yet, higher education seems to continually want to climb, and climb again and yet again. And then just allow ourselves to fall off the flagpole, so we can start all over every semester, quarter or start period. I don't know about you, but I have always found that falling leads to pain, hurt, scraped knees and having to exert extra energy and resources to pick myself up and start all over again.

It is a simple truth that if a college focuses on retaining the students and the employees it had recruited, the school will be more successful in every aspect of its operations. From teaching to its finances and even its ability to attract grants, research and alumni dollars.

Our research shows that most attrition, drops, step-outs, whatever you wish to call them leave a school because of reasons that fall directly into the category of customer service. Maybe not customer service as you might read about in one of the corporate or commercial improve-your-sales customer service books. But, customer service for higher education as it must be defined for the activities, traditions, attitudes, folkways, mores, codes and people of the academic environment. Customer service for that unique and distinctive world we know as higher education. But customer service nonetheless. And improving it at a school can have enormous effects on everything from retention and revenue to morale and mission.

The key to retention is providing good customer service to the customer, or in the case of schools, its client students. Note I didn't even say excellent service or come through with any of those business clichés or catch phrases like *Service beyond Service* or *Customer Service that Pops.* Nope.

Why not?

Because colleges are indeed businesses. But quite different businesses from a Starbucks or Nordstrom's or even Disneyland, though some may find parallels in some of the things we do if we but just adjust some terms as stated in my earlier book *Embrace the Oxymoron: Customer Service in Higher Education* (LRP Publications: 2002).

"Colleges are starting to see higher education in business-like realities. They are realizing that revenue depends on selling the college (recruitment) to its customers (students and parents). Sales (enrollment) are made based on the college's brand (image), product (courses, programs, degrees), and by creating a connection with the customer (customer service)."

But even recognizing the business aspects of academia, colleges are also unlike most stores, commercial enterprises or vacation spots in what they *sell*, the services they provide and the buying events they create for their students, their customers. Stores seek to make sales of items, of merchandise. These are one time, one day events in which a store attempts to attract and retain a customer long enough in its building to make a sale of items or deliver a service before the customer leaves the premises. They also try to provide a level of attention that will encourage the customer to buy as much as possible during the buying event and perhaps come back again when they need more or a different product. Colleges do not sell items as such. They should not set out to create a unique, one time sales occasion to get students to buy as large as possible a group of products or services when they are in the buildings on campus or before they leave that day. Though it can be successfully argued that we do provide both product and service to our clients, our students, we are not there to supply a singular commodity like a cup of coffee or a product like a pair of pants or a blouse. Certainly, not a weekend or even a week-long vacation or event in which you can forget about the world and meet Goofy.

Students are both the raw material and the consumers of our enterprise, our businesses, and our schools. The increased value and ability of our students, our customers, is our real business. For more commercial enterprises, the customer is a means to an end. For us, they are the means and the end.

The primary goal of a Starbucks, Nordstrom's, Disney or even a dollar store is primarily focused on making money. They need customers to do that. Good schools, even good for-profit schools are focused primarily on educating students and generating knowledge and training so our customers can succeed. We know that if our graduates succeed, we have succeeded.

And the school's revenues are tied to those goals. Students in school paying tuition generate to a college's revenue. Yes, we also need to have revenue to run the school, pay bills, educate students and afford faculty, staff and even administrators. But money is not the primary motivation of most schools. There are some one may wonder about but they are the anomaly, not the rule. That is not to say that every school does not seek to develop a fund balance or surplus funds which may also be called a profit or margin. But in most schools, profit is not the primary or sole operative mode. Having enough revenue to pay the bills and operate the school to meet its mission and goals is indeed an operational necessity. And it can definitely be helped by making certain we always have enough students and tuitions to accomplish the budget goals and needs. But almost all colleges and universities worthy of the label higher educational institutions do not provide their services solely in pursuit of cash flow, margins and profit.

What we provide our customers is a multiplicity of intangibles like thoughts, ideas, learning, intelligence, skills, possibilities and potential. Products and commodities of the brain, emotions and hands that cannot be held, touched, worn, seen, smelled or tasted. The merchandise of higher education is the student him or herself and his or her greater worth and value after interacting with the institution, its people, services and products.

This is also what the people who work at the school expect and deserve. After all, people do not work at the school for the high pay and short hours. They work at the college because they feel they can make a difference. They too expect to be treated with value and importance. They have a right to anticipate they will not just provide service but will be provided good service themselves. What is said for students can apply for everyone on campus.

The Way to Do That – Customer Service

Customer service in a college is not just smiling, pandering and playing at caring like a waiter at a chain restaurant with *please, thank you* and *come again* to elicit a tip. Faculty do not introduce themselves with "Hi I'm Doctor Wendy, and I will be your intellectual server today. Can I start you off with a syllabus?" Though after nine years of working with colleges to improve their customer service, I have to admit that for some schools artificial smiles, and a superficial veneer of etiquette and caring would be a real plus.

Customer service in academia does include providing the genuine service of educating and training the client for the future. It includes treating students and one another as if they have enduring value and importance. It means that everyone in the community is a customer or a client of one another, and we are all dedicated to serving as if we all were Rotarians – *Service Above Self.* Furthermore, it means doing all we can to assure the customers have all the instruction, tools and assistance needed to be able to obtain the final service they came to college to obtain. And what is that final service? Graduation, the diploma, the certification that is required to move to the next step of their lives – a job or graduate school – and the career assistance to get there. That is what the student is finally paying for and expects, so that certainly must be a major focus of collegiate customer service.

Or perhaps I should say graduation *should* be a major focus because it is not in many schools. It may even be fair and accurate to say this about most schools. How do we know? Just look at the six-year bachelor degree national graduation rates at most colleges and universities from 2000-2006. The national average graduation rate for students after six years of attending and paying tuition and fees is a feeble 56.4%.

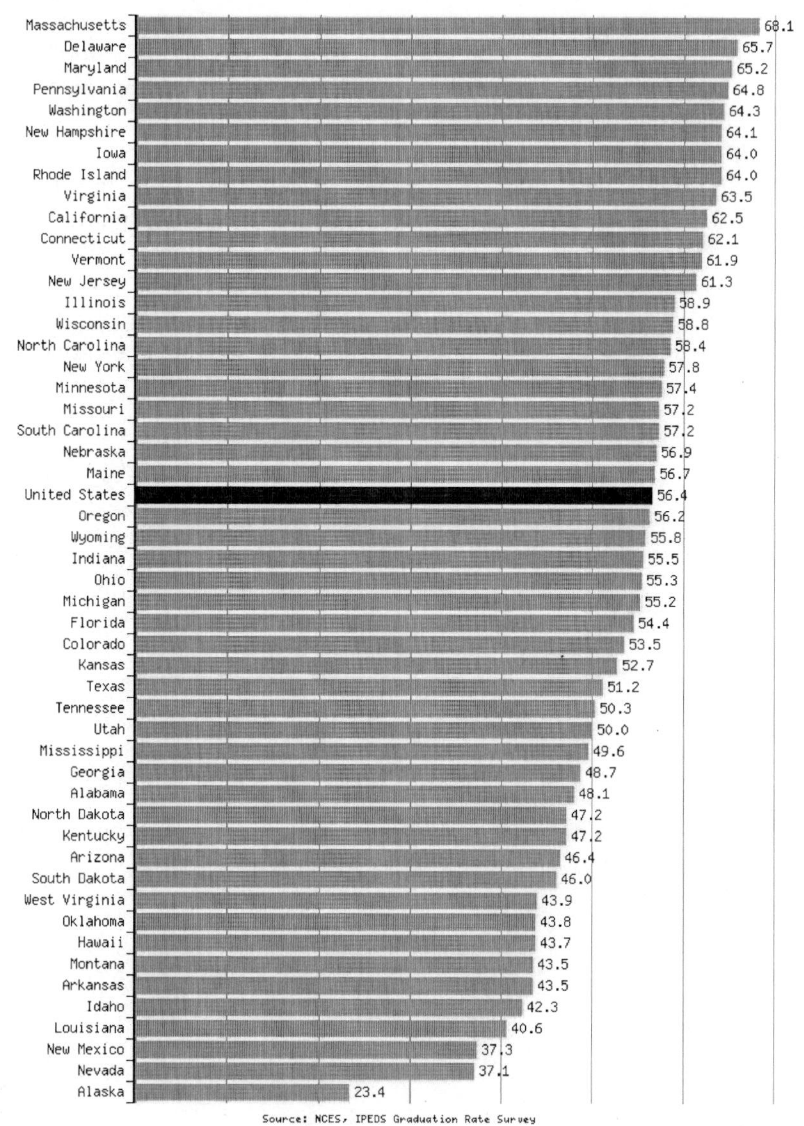

That means that just under half of all the students who attend college do not graduate that school or maybe any school. That is an appalling statistic. It means also that the average college or university is losing most of its students. That also translates to almost half of its potential revenue walking out the door as shown in the NCHEMS data below. It also translates as a serious drain on fund raising. Odd things, people who do not graduate do not become alumni donors.

Even worse for the ethos of a college, when a school loses so many potential graduates, it also loses its ability to meet its natural core mission of providing undergraduate education to strengthen individuals and the collective future.

What is your school's graduation rate? Check out the persistence to graduation rates. Look at the way colleges do not schedule to assure courses are offered so graduation can be accomplished in four years. Contemplate the decline in services such as counseling, advising and retention that affect graduation and student success. Getting students to their primary goal – leaving the college with a diploma – should not be just a primary focus of the students but also of the administration, faculty or staff on most campuses. If it is not, there are going to be service, mission and revenue issues at the college.

The 72% Factor

Customer service issues account for as much as 72% of all attrition. When we interviewed students who left one school for another or simply dropped completely out of postsecondary education, we found the bottom line reasons for leaving went to issues such as the school's indifference to them; not feeling valued; rude, unsympathetic, non-responsive or unfriendly staff, faculty or administrators; a general feeling which can be encapsulated in the oft heard phrase, "All they cared about was my money."

These are what we have found as the three major reasons why students left their schools.

Reason	Percentage
School was indifferent toward me	30%
Staff issues	29%
Just Plain Unhappy	13%
TOTAL	**72%**

These are all customer service issues. And all are valid reasons for losing enrollment and revenue, because if a student feels a school does not care about him or her, it doesn't. And that sense of not caring is a common feeling for the 72% who drop out due to weak or ineffectual customer service.

Through improving customer service a school will increase its success and its fiscal situation. For example, if a school increased its retention by 50%, it could recoup a sizable amount of admissions and recruitment costs that could go to other important aspects of the school's function – like more full-time faculty, new equipment, more clerical staff, providing all those adjuncts a decent wage and maybe even some benefits, replacing cancelled library acquisitions, maybe even lessening the length of the deferred maintenance list on campus.

What is even more striking than the costs that could be saved are the possibilities of freezing or even reducing tuition and fees, morale going up, happier faculty, clerical, administrators and trustees is the fact that the school could have the revenue it needs to operate and meet its strategic mission along with academic objectives and goals. With a fuller revenue stream, a school would actually be able to focus more fully on its mission and educational passion better. And that would be a benefit for everyone in the college community – faculty, staff, administrators and most importantly, the students – the real business of higher education.

This can all be accomplished through effective customer service and focusing on retention at least as much as, if not more than, the acquisition of more new students.

With a better understanding of collegiate customer service and some simple ways to improve it, it becomes easier and very beneficial to all involved to keep a customer rather than to obtain another two or three new ones to replace a dropout. To keep the students sitting in classes rather than going through the effort of convincing yet another potential student to climb that flagpole of recruitment..

Yes, I do realize and accept that research is an important part of the mission of many college and universities. That is a simple fact of higher education in the current times. But research is not the most important factor. It is not why society and government support colleges. It may be why corporations and even some college personnel are supportive of certain institutions because they make money from university research. But what drives the external support is that colleges educate the future for our society, economy and our sons and daughters.

The public expects a college to focus on its students as the primary purpose for the school's being. That is what voters support in a millage or tax increase for a school. A family does not pay tens of thousands of dollars in tuition, fees and expenses to support research and have its child get an inferior education and experience. Society and students' families expect that the learning and preparation of students for productive, economically strong and rewarding lives for the individual and all of society is the primary purpose of a university.

If a university were to announce it was doing away with undergraduate education to focus on research, how much support other than from some self-serving corporations do you think it would obtain? Likely not very much.

Should a school also expect that if students are not treated as the most important aspect of the college it will retain support? Or should it plan to lose students if it loses focus on the students?

Obviously it should expect to have retention issues if it does not attend to academic customer service concerns. Academic but not retail customer service approaches. They really do not work well in academia. But what are the differences?

Customer service? For academia?

Just what in the world is it really?

Maybe it's like art. We may not know why a picture is great or not, but we can feel it when it is or isn't within our reactions to it. Brushstrokes, colors, perspective, shadows, light, artistic feeling and passion. For each of us finally it is most often an emotional response that defies explanation except by a critic or consultant. There is just something about it that makes you feel it is artistic and maybe even art.

Perhaps it's the enigmatic smile of Mona Lisa, the inscrutable power of a Rothko, the shadow and light of *The Night Watch* – that lovely use of light as the moon reflects off the church steeple to illuminate the snowy village or even the look on the puppy's face with the eyes that follow you across the room. Wait a minute. The last couple of pictures mentioned? Are they art? Maybe yes maybe no. It might well depend on who is defining art and looking at the picture. One might suppose the faculty of a university art department could have a different definition than a buyer seeking a painting for a living room for example.

And customer service? Is it like art? Could be. It is also quite much like love I think. You just know when it exists. When you have felt it. And when you haven't. Even more, when it is not there or gone and you should go also.

Most experts will tell you customer service is a process of focusing so fully on meeting the satisfaction level of the customer, that he or she will love you and want to come back when he or she needs another item you sell. Others will say it is loving the customer – hugging them, embracing them, (depending on the business, this is usually metaphoric in nature) overwhelming them with service. That'll make them love you back and buy from you. The old *the customer is always right* notion.
Yet others will say that it is a series of activities that will make the customer more than happy with dealing and buying from you. Others propose that customer service is providing the customer service beyond service. That is often the basis of the commercial books on customer service. Collections of anecdotes abound about people who go the extra ten or twenty miles to return a keychain or some such trivial item and of people who did something extraordinary to please a customer followed by exhortations to do something extraordinary.

Almost as if the customers were royalty as in the days of kings. And the customer is the king – not a peasant, which is reportedly how most people believe they are treated nowadays according to what I hear and read about service. Roll out the red carpet. Blow a trumpet fanfare of greeting followed by a low bow from the waist and an obsequious, "Welcome to…" And then do everything to make the king happy. Never disappoint. Don't even think of a frown or disagreeing with the queen. "Your wish is my command," and think of what they want even before they think of it. If the customer says jump, your only question is how high. Do whatever is possible to make them happy. Make them feel special and important. Now that's customer service!

Not only is that not real customer service in commercial enterprises, it could never and possibly should never be found in higher education. These actions focus on the surface process and perhaps even pandering. They overlook the value of the product; the service provided and the return on investment customers and students expect. Customer service for higher education must have more profundity in its actions and results. It must also be more meaningful, sincere and found not in surface actions but in the deeper obligation of teaching, learning and human growth and potential. It is a service geared to the students' goals, their major areas of study, the acquisition of skills needed to succeed in life and career. A one process fits all will not meet every students' needs and expectations.

The Rules of Working Here

Rule 1: The customer is always right.
Rule 2: Any questions? Consult rule 1.

Recently a faculty member told me that teaching introductory courses had become more of a battle against indifference, ringing cell phones, blatant disrespect such as sleeping in class and students wandering in and out at will. I told her some of these problems can be solved quickly by demanding the respect she and the profession deserve by not allowing such behaviors. Her response was "Yuh, right. Like the administration is going to let me." She strongly believed she would not be supported in an effort to require and demand decorum in the classroom. The administration, she said, "wanted to boost retention numbers so it set forward a customer service effort."

"We are supposed to be aware of the customer and his or her happiness or something like that. And as we know, customers are always right. Just give 'em a few assignments, high grades and keep 'em happy."

As a customer service consultant for colleges indulge me when I assure you that first, this is, to use technical administrative term BALONEY.

First, is the customer always right?

Second, is what she described really customer service?

And, third, any so-called customer service effort based on easy grades and coddling students will fail and create more problems than it will solve.

Is the customer always right? This old adage has been held up as a simple truth for 100 years. But should it be? It began as a different phrase attributed to César Ritz, the owner of the Ritz Hotel in Paris. In 1908 Ritz is supposed to have told his staff *Le client n'a jamais tort* – *The customer is never wrong.* More than likely, he was just trying to make a point with his Parisian staff to not treat the customers as a rudely as Parisians are famous for doing. The *never wrong* aspect came into the phrase as it did because as Stephen Clarke points out in the title of the first chapter of his book *Talk to the Snail* (Bloomsbury, 2006) "Thou Shalt Be Wrong (if you're not French)". . Clarke continues,

> When dealing with a Frenchman, you need to be aware that there is a voice in his head. It is constantly telling him, *I'm French. I'm right.*

And keep in mind that since the hotel was in Paris, the center of the French universe, the Parisians that worked at the Ritz likely considered themselves more right than their non-Parisian French guests. And they not only may have enjoyed insulting the rubes from the frontier, they also may have felt it was their job and right to do so.

What Monsieur Ritz was trying to get across to his staff was, "Do not treat our paying guests as idiots who do not know anything, do not correct them and do not point out their inferiority because they are not from here. Pretend they are not incorrect". César Ritz was not saying the customers were right or correct. *Mais non.* He had to keep in mind that the guests were not Parisians after all. He was telling the hotel staff to just not point out that the guests are necessarily wrong. Overlook their inferiority and the hotel will make more money from repeat stays.

The phrase we know and should forget was Americanized and next attributed to Marshall Field in Chicago. Even he was not saying the customer could not be wrong but to treat the customer as if he or she were special, welcome and of the right type to shop in our store. Marshall Field's was an elegant store and Mr. Field wanted everyone to feel welcome and valued there, even if they were not among the Chicago elite. As if they were important and of the *right* class. He did not want customers to feel out of place or second-rate. After all, their money was revenue too.

But in the American drive to simplify (if it is not a federal document) we rewrote the phrase. We went beyond and made it into a business adage that gave it more power than it was ever meant to have. We actually thought the phrase meant the customer could not be wrong. Do anything to make them happy and feel right. Treat them as if they were commercial royalty. Not the original intent and not what any college should ever try to do.

The Customer is... ?

Oh, you want the $60 pants for $10...?

You wore the socks for a week and now want to return them?

You liked the lobster but wish to only pay $5 for the meal?

I know I wasn't in class much, missed the exams and didn't complete assignments, but I still would like an A.

As they say in New Jersey: *fugedaboudit.*

It has been an inviolable adage found in most customer service books that tell readers that both rules number 1 and number 2 are correct. The customer is always right.

It is therefore our role to do all we can to please the customer; to make her feel we accept that she and her business are number one to the store or institution by fulfilling every wish if at all possible; to go the extra mile to make the customer happy; to indulge, pamper, spoil and if necessary, to even pander to each whim to assure the customer is satisfied and will come back.

It is this time honored yet false dictum that is so strongly at odds with the academic beliefs of many people on college campuses. Influential segments of the college community believe the adage that the customer is right imposes a construct of business on a very non-commercial institution – academia. It is construed as a basic bastard of business which has money as its goal being forced upon intellectual institutions with ideals of intellectual pursuit and learning, in that order. Obviously not just a mismatch but an attempt to undermine the very nature of the academic environment and *corporatize* the academy as one faculty member told me prior to a workshop he refused to attend. Colleges and universities are not about money and revenue after all.

In fact, money corrupts the purity of the intellectual community, except when it comes to my office or department's budget perhaps. Or my salary, benefit cost or equipment. But then the money is only needed to be able to provide education or services to others to make the institution stronger to be better able to meet its mission. And after all, we do not have customers. Students are not customers. They are....students. So I don't pick number 1 or 2.

Students do pay for an education so they must be customers, and we should listen to business to make sure the revenue comes in. After all, without money coming in how are we to fund your budget, pay for salary and benefit increases and all the other things we need to meet the mission. So we need to consider that number 1 may have some merit. Perhaps we need an ad hoc committee to study...

Save us all from even one more committee! Let's just realize that in typical academic mode, the positions are all or nothing postures that are both wrong and yet still right.

Consider that if you checked number 1 as correct, number 2 necessarily follows as acceptable. But if you chose number 1as true, you are wrong to begin with. The customer is not always right. Yet, that does not make the faculty member who derided customer service as illegitimate in higher education right. Not at all, for he is also wrong. Very palpably wrong at that. And in this case, your wrong and his wrong do not make the customer right.

The reality is that the customer is often wrong. Particularly in higher education. Just think of your last quiz. I am sure you found many students were wrong in many of their answers or guesses. That is the nature of a quiz or a test after all. Though we would hope that the customer would be always right and prove that he or she really understood the lectures, the readings and the assignments, such is not the reality of most classes and schools. Students, our customers, are often wrong. (Actually so is the term *customer* for our students, but that will be discussed in another section.)

The reality is that students are wrong by their very nature as students. They come to college to learn what they do not know; to become more correct in their knowledge and abilities. They are in school to replace erroneous or uninformed notions with information and learning. In fact, if they already knew, if they had the skills prior to coming into school, they would not have to enroll. They would not become students, our clients and customers.

What Is Customer Service in College?

Wrong by Their Very Nature as Students

Most business people know the adage is at the very least overstated and many realize it is actually untrue even as they keep posting it in the backrooms and employee break rooms. They want to get the sense that the customer is important and valuable out to employees. They don't want the employees treating customers as they have been treated elsewhere. The customer is not always right. They are in fact, often wrong. But the issue is actually not right or wrong but how one goes about letting them know they are wrong. Or as the fortune cookie said, "Diplomacy is telling someone to go to hell and having them ask for directions."

This is especially true in an academic environment. The customer is most often at least somewhat wrong, and that's why they take classes and listen to us. We theoretically give tests and quizzes to find out how much students have learned and what they have not learned. By finding out what they got wrong students can then learn, gain more intelligence and abilities, and then correct their errors. By discovering what students know and don't know, teachers can also learn what they may not have taught as well as they could have and spend time clarifying the information to the benefit of learning...or so the pedagogical theory goes.

Pointing out incorrectness is supposed to lead to a salutary effect for both student and teacher. Though too often we just use tests and quizzes to set a score and thus justify as grade. But we surely realize that we cannot just give everyone 100% on tests and A's for grades because the student/customer is never wrong.

We should recognize that students being wrong, having faulty or incomplete information, or having limits to their knowledge and/or abilities is central to the very nature of the teaching/learning process. Students come to us knowing they do not know and to find out even more of what they do not know so they can obtain that knowledge, skills and/or training to learn and grow to be able to obtain the job and career they seek. The process of learning is the replacing of wrongs, limits, intellectual inadequacies and unfocused, obtuse, even just plain dumb ideas or ignorance with knowledge, truth, abilities and skills. As a result, it is our job to teach them that they are wrong at times and replace what they don't have right. They simply cannot always be right. To do that, we have to allow them to be wrong.

As such, we need to stop thinking of students as customers. Students really are not customers, consumers, guests or any of the other myriad commercial terms businesses use for the people to whom they are trying to sell things. They are really something else.

Clients. Not customers.

They are not coming to us to buy a shirt, or skirt or IPhone or any retail goods or anything material at all. They are after an intangible. Students come to school to obtain education, knowledge, improvement and growth. And most importantly, the certification they will need to get to the job or next step in their lives.

They are incomplete individuals who are intellectually weak or ill in a sense. They go to school and classes to learn how to make themselves stronger and sounder. They come to higher education realizing they are incomplete and intellectually weak beings that have to learn how to strengthen mind and body to be able to run and compete in the marathon of career and adult life. As if higher education were a large clinic filled with specialists who will help them find out what is wrong with them. Then provide them answers, remedies and prescriptions that will make them better and stronger. As if faculty were intellectual physicians.

Actually, students and faculty/staff of colleges can fall readily into the patient-doctor/client relationship quite nicely.

Patients/clients come to an expert/doctor to have the expert study their needs, weaknesses, strengths and then tell them what needs to be done and guide them to resolve a condition or improve their situation. We do the same in a college. Just as a doctor will diagnose a patient and then tell him/her what course of action needs to be followed to become healthy and meet the patient's goals, even if it is bad news, we do the same in the learning/teaching process. We begin by diagnosing student knowledge and skills. Then determine a course of action and rehabilitation that are designed to help the students become intellectually healthier and fitter for future growth. Then the faculty check on the patient's progress, chart it and determine what next steps can and should be taken. So faculty are not just doctors in title but in action. Though as my wife so rightly informed me when I received my PhD. "Dr. Walker the OBGYN guy can deliver babies. You? Only speeches."

So then what does customer service mean for a doctor and a classroom professor? Is there a good side-armchair-manner that PhD doctors should be aware of to be successful with their patients in a class? Yes there is.

Alice B. Burkin, a leading medical malpractice specialist at the Boston law firm of Duane Morris, LLP, has researched what makes a doctor less likely to be sued and more likely to be successful with patients. The major thing the successful physicians do, which also makes them less likely to be sued for malpractice even when they might have committed it, is treat patients as valuable individuals and indicate that they really do care about them.

Another aspect of their personality is an important one. They are not arrogant. They say hello. They listen to patients, listen to their answers and answer all of their questions. They explain the condition or course of treatment in lay terms so patients can understand. They are human and personable. They enlist the patients in the process and care. They indicate to the patients that they actually care about them as an individual and not as a co-pay keeping them from yet another co-pay. And that caring means assessing their real needs and telling them the truth. Even when the truth is painful.

Even when they came in because they thought they had a bug and it turns out be much more than that. If the doctor followed the *always right* dictum, she would just tell them they were right, "It is just the flu." I would suppose anyone would agree that this would neither be right nor good customer service especially when the situation is much worse but curable if the patient knows the truth and follows the prescribed remedy. Telling the patient he is wrong and this is what he must do even if he does not wish to do so is an example of what would be excellent customer service.

What is good customer service for medical doctors also works as in-class customer service for professors. Faculty and all members of the community should begin by caring about the students. Do not expect them to all be brilliant and care about your subject or what you do. They likely may not. They may actually be taking the course being taught because they have to take it. Just as we all had required courses we could neither stand nor see as valuable, so will students in your institution. But as the good medical doctor would do, explain to the students why the subject matter is important, not just intellectually, but to them, to their well-being, to their future and life. For example, when I taught composition at a maritime college, I started by assigning the students to write a job application letter. When they received them back and I explained why the XYZ Company could not hire someone who has poor grammar, awkward sentence structure, weak word choice, unclear or awkward sentences because log entries and things like damage reports must be precise and correct or there could be major problems, they started to get the idea.

They were never really thrilled, maybe not even moderately happy about having to take composition but they saw some value and did work at improving their writing. But then, I recognized and accepted that reality as well as the fact that these technical school students actually had very little knowledge of grammar, sentence structure, punctuation or even spelling. But I knew that going in and set my expectations at the same level a medical doctor would when prescribing therapy. They know most patients will not follow instructions precisely, so they overstate hoping to obtain at least enough compliance with treatment to help the patient become healthier. This is especially so if the treatment or the prescription is painful or not all that pleasant. Sort of like learning grammar and structure for my first year mariners.

If a professor would do the same at the start of a class, it may help keep him or her from getting upset when students are neither all that interested nor knowledgeable about the subject being taught. That they are not excited about the course should not be surprising to anyone. They really do not know about it yet. It is the faculty member's job to get them energized on the topics (okay maybe just attentive) so they will learn the subject. If they knew the information or skill coming in, they would not need the class or the faculty member after all.

This is also true for school administrators or staff. Most students will never be as excited as you may be about some regulation, procedure or rule the student has broken or overlooked. Students usually have no real interest in them as can be seen by how very few of them ever read any of them inside the catalog whose accuracy we sweated over, reviewed and checked before giving it to them. So, be a doctor to them. Explain in terms they understand and resolve a course of action.

And most important, do not be arrogant. It is the arrogant doctors who lose patients and malpractice suits. And it is the arrogant professors who lose their students, their interest and respect. It is only on this issue, response to arrogance that the customer is always right.

Just as the good, less likely to be sued medical doctor, we must be amiable, professionally personable with students. Learn their names. Find out who they are. Get a full write-up on them. Maybe faculty could even start the class each semester as a doctor would with an information sheet to learn more about them, their knowledge in the subject, any anxieties they bring to the class so the professor can teach and remedy their needs even better. For administrators, get them talking. Take notes and use what is said to examine the issue before determining a remedy. And never be like one of the doctors who do not care. Do not stop listening or jump to a conclusion about the case. Just as bad doctors make bad diagnoses from not listening, so will you. That's how doctors lose patients and schools lose students.

The customer is always right and other failed concepts from business should not be transferred to academia. Customer service must be a priority on campuses today as we work with a student body that expects it. But, it must be done right. And that is quite different from the customer being right.

In order to be able to fulfill their obligations to the patient/student, the doctor and professor must retain control over the examination and session. The patient is there to be helped and must be an active participant in the process but the expert must be in control. If a patient is unruly or unmanageable, the examination will be curtailed and the patient asked to leave. The doctor will neither allow herself to make a wrong diagnosis nor allow other patients to have their care harmed. If a patient checks himself out of the hospital, a doctor will most often suggest the patient not come back to the practice. As for cell phones, most doctors tell patients to shut them off when they come in the office.

So in the classroom, the faculty member should act like an intellectual/training doctor. If a student checks him or herself out of the class without authorization, that student is not allowed back into the class that day and maybe in the future. Rude or unacceptable behavior is just that and does not belong. Do not allow disruptive behavior just as a doctor would not permit it in an examining room or a ward, for it will harm the other students. And cell phones are not allowed.

That by the way is actually good customer service. Especially when we accept that the customer is not always right but our job is to make them righter even if the medicine may not taste good.

Pogo is Right Again

A faculty member of a client college I had presented a workshop at last year emailed today. Seems he was confused. He is getting fed up with the way students behave in class. He said he is tired of competing with cell phones; upset by students who just walk into or out of class when they feel like it and certainly bored and even appalled at times by the language, tone ands attitude some students use. He feels he should not allow these sorts of activities but is concerned that would go against what the *customer service attitudes* being expressed by his department chair which fears a high dropout percentage. Fewer students could lead to a smaller budget? Those attitudes are expressed by supporting students who might complain the faculty member is being too hard or strict in class. The faculty member comes up for tenure soon and does not want any problems.

Okay, leaving the whole tenure process and results on teaching and student service aside because that is one of the largest problems in academia, what the faculty member described is a common misunderstanding. But I must say that the faculty member and his chair just prove the Pogo cartoon once again.

We have met the enemy and they are us!

If anyone believes that pandering to the worst instincts and behaviors of students is providing customer service they are not only wrong, but to quote Dr. House, "They are idiots." They are not providing good customer service anymore than a dentist who sees a bad tooth and leaves it in so as not to cause the patient pain from a root canal.

Keep in mind that anyone who has the misguided belief that the academic customer is always right is almost always wrong. QUIZZES ANYONE?

Students are not right. In fact it is because they are wrong – or maybe a better word, flawed – that they come to college. They attend higher education because they know they are not prepared to succeed in a career yet. They also realize they need to learn from books and from people if they are to get that job or grad school before a job to reach their goals in life. They pay money to be made stronger, smarter and less socially awkward. And due to false notions of customer service we fail them – sometimes in all three areas.

If we make courses easier because we believe they do not want to work that hard, that is not customer service. If we do not challenge them as much as we ought to create greater intellectual plasticity and ability preferring to hand out high grades that will reinforce their self-esteem, we have not served them well. And if we allow them to act in ways in our classes that will surely get them fired on a job, we have failed. That is not customer service! That is in fact, major disservice.

If anyone believes that letting students skip classes will be helpful to them in the world of work, it can only be an academic living in the tenured palace. There is no right to fail in life. Faculty who allow students to walk in late or walk out when they want, talk on the phone, nap during class, be rude, use inappropriate language, be rude to the teacher, hand in homework when and if they please and so on are just preparing these students for failure in life. And they are preparing themselves to hate what they are doing as teachers.

"Uh, Ms. Dennison, I came into the meeting late because I really needed a latte, and I had to leave the meeting to talk to my bud who is having a rough time right now. Oh yuh, the analysis you need and told me to get to you today, well, I had stuff to do so I didn't get it done yet, but I may be able to get to after some things I need to do tonight. Okay?"

How long will that graduate of your college have that job I wonder?

By letting students act in inappropriate ways that will bite them in the future is so far from good customer service that it is appallingly bad. College is not just to instruct on some facts, some processes. It is to teach some abilities to survive and thrive in the real world. Real customer service is telling students who walk in late, "You just got fired from your job and class today. Arriving late and interrupting me and the class is unacceptable behavior which will not be tolerated here or in whatever field of work you wish to enter."

"Cell phones are not permitted to be used in this class. It is disrespectful to me and your classmates when you talk during class and will not be accepted by your colleagues nor your bosses on a job. Shut them off. Leave them off during this class."

"Work is due when it is due. If it is not on time, there will be consequences here as there would be on the job you may eventually get."

And so on. You get the idea. Taking positions such as those above is actually good customer/client service. Moreover, it is also providing good academic customer service to the other students who are trying to learn from you. They are as upset with interruptions, cell calls, talking, sleeping, etc. as you are. Maybe even more so. They are not paying for you to let other students hinder their chances to learn and succeed.

Students are your clients who come to your school and your class to be made better and stronger just as any client with a problem, a challenge or a need comes to an expert. We expect the expert to tell us the truth and to tell us what needs to be done even if it is not necessarily what we ant to hear. Just as when I am a client of my doctor I expect the truth and courses of action with integrity even if I do not want to watch what I eat or how I exercise.

Would anyone feel he or she received good service if the doctor told us that we were engaged in unhealthy behaviors and should just keep doing them? "Hey, I don't want to upset you," you know bedside manner and all, "so yes keep drinking to excess, overeating fried and fatty foods topped with ice cream and candy, engaging in a sedentary lifestyle, sticking nickels in your nose, coming to class late unprepared and overtired, talking on the cell phone during meetings, cursing out your boss and just being a general pain in the butt is just fine. And oh yes, while you're at it, you might consider smoking too. Keep it up."

Of course not. And we should not be doing anything even close to that in the name of customer service. We do not help students, and we certainly do not help ourselves. Stop it and replace it with real service. Being a provider of good customer service does not mean doing what is harmful to the students now and for the future.

Durgin Park

I went to a very popular restaurant in the Haymarket section of Boston. This particular restaurant has been around since 1827. To be around that long in the tough restaurant business, Durgin Park must know how to do things right. The restaurant must be a paragon of service. An example to all others. And in its own way, for Durgin Park, I suppose it is.

After my guest and I arrived, we had to stand in a long line and wait for a seat, not a table, as waitresses rushed and pushed around the customers with both hands and mouths. "Hey, move over. I'm working here!" one said as she cut in front of me. "Out of my way," another cursed as she carried a tray of food through the line of customers waiting to be seated. Hmmm, with this sort of service, how could this place not only be recommended but have all these people waiting for a seat? People have been nicer to me in a bursar's office during collection calls.

After a wait of about twenty minutes, we were finally seated. And I do mean seated. We were shown to chairs but not at our own table. We were put at a long communal table, sort of like the old television show with the multi-generational Walton family gathering around their long dining room table with benches on either side. It was like that but without the friendliness of family. We were stuck between other couples we did not know. And we did not get to know them or the other couples gathered around the shared table that night. Not quite the homey ending of the Walton's with everyone in the family saying goodnight to one another.

A waitress finally came over to take our order. It took a little while. "Okay what'll it be?" she requested.

I am a notoriously slow decider in restaurants because I generally want to try everything on the menu. In fact, I took so long at one place that my father-in-law became impatient and barked, "Choose something already!" I made the mistake of then ordering the first thing I saw. Meatloaf. As a result, I do all I can not to be rushed. After all, I don't like meatloaf. So I told the waitress I would need a minute or two. "Okay but not too much longer. We're real busy tonight." And she walked off.

The meal came without ceremony. It actually was quite good, especially the Indian pudding for dessert. The pot roast I got was quite fine and tender. Equally important, there was enough to fill me up. I am a person of dependably large appetite. But the waitress? WOW!

And not in a good customer service way. I had not been treated like that in a long time even in some of the *greasy spoon* places I often frequent while on the road. Not even in a union negotiating meeting over a contentious contract. Never mind no. "Hi my name is Tiffany. I'll be your server tonight. May I push drinks at you?" No server had ever grumbled openly at me before in a restaurant. At least not to my face! I had to wait over ten minutes for another napkin after mine hit the floor and I requested a replacement. Refilled water glasses? If I wanted to get the water it seemed I had to work at getting the server's attention to get it. Getting a refill on coffee to go with the Indian pudding I fortunately chose for dessert?

Would we ever go back to Durgin Park? A place where the service was so bad, the waitresses so very rude and where we even had to share a picnic table with strangers? After all, Durgin Park broke almost all the rules of great service according to most every book and expert on good service. A few rules of terrible service came into being it seemed too. I mean we all know that restaurants with poor service can't last. As a customer service consultant I would be required to tell Durgin Park that if they keep that up, there is no way they can succeed. No way can they last.

How long have they been getting away with that sort of service and stayed in business? Food service is a very competitive business. And with such poor customer service, I doubt if they can keep it going any more than maybe another year before the tourists find out. Okay, well maybe five. Ten years tops if they keep paying off the hotel concierges who send them new out-of-towners. Perhaps they can live off their reputation for maybe 10 more. But their reputation – Famously poor service – kept them in business for what? Just 180 years so far. Clearly their service has limited them to merely 180 years of success. So what's history tell us then? Another 180 years. Well maybe. But only if they straighten out. Or actually, maybe if they don't.

Hi I'm Don. I'll Be Your Insulter Tonight

Maybe what I overheard about Durgin Park later the same night will help clarify.

While walking off the meal, I overheard another couple talking about their experience at Durgin Park that night. They were a bit upset it seemed. One could hear it in their complaints. "Wonder what is happening there? I mean who do they think we are? Tourists? Hicks from the Midwest?"

"That waitress we got stuck with. Please and thank you all night. The food came quickly. She checked my water glass… I mean what the hell was the matter with her? I don't know. Maybe the place is just changing. And not for the better either. I'll give it the food, as usual, was great. That prime rib was huge, tender and very tasty. Especially for the money. Oh, did you remember the doggy bag? Good. Well, I guess we'll give it another shot the next time we're in the city. But I hope we get a normal Durgin Park waitress next time."

Huh? They missed getting bad service as most experts would define it? They were disappointed with good service and a polite and attentive waitress? What goes on here? Durgin Park is breaking the customer service rules and being rewarded for it? They would go back if they could be insulted and ignored? This does not seem to make sense.

But wait a minute. I didn't go there for the legendary great service. The couple I overheard while walking around actually expected somewhat rude and impolite waitresses as part of the Durgin Park experience. And I got what I anticipated. The service was just part of the show I expected.

Would I go back? Of course! Great food at a decent price and with service that was absolutely service below service! What I finally realize is I wasn't really buying the service itself. Certainly not. It was the food that was really most important to me after all. I'd rather have great food and bad service than great service and bad food. I am paying for the food. The tip is the payment for the service. Now if the service were good enough to match the food, maybe that would have been an even nicer experience. But not necessarily the Durgin Park experience.

It's sort of like paying to see Don Rickles or Kathy Griffiths. If I went to see their show and they weren't what some would consider nasty, even offensive at times, I would feel as if I did not get my money's worth. If either of them came out, told mild, safe jokes and did not make fun of people, I would be very dissatisfied. I would not have gotten what I had paid for, the full value of the investment of time, money and emotion I made in them. On the other hand, if I went into a store and the person at the cash register started doing Rickles all over me, I might be upset unless I was getting a great bargain or an item I really wanted badly enough to inconvenience myself. Like the people who waited to buy I-Phones or waited in line for hours to get the last Harry Potter book. They were being treated poorly, at least indifferently at many stores, but would only complain if the phone didn't work or the book was weak.

So a Durgin Park with good, plentiful food, reasonable prices for the amount and quality of food, long tables of strangers, and rude waitresses is the Durgin Park I went there for. Now if the food was not so good and the service was what I got…that's a different story. Wouldn't go back. After all, it is finally the food itself that determines the continuing value of a restaurant.

McService

Just think of the times you went to eat and got great service. Top notch waiter. Great ambience. But the food was horrible. Dried out. Tasteless, tiny portions. Going to rush back there for the service and bad food? Don't think so. Now if the food is good but not great, selection is varied, the service okay, and the price reasonable, might just go back there. How else does one explain a buffet after all? There is no real service. If you're lucky someone comes and removes dirty plates as they pile up. You are the service at a buffet. But the prices are usually reasonable. Food quite varied. Plentiful. Sometimes even good. So we go back and serve ourselves. Sort of like registration at most universities.

Or if the place is very well-known, extremely impressive reputation, quite hard to get into, quite expensive, service attitude consciously ranging from *You should be happy I am willing to serve you* to apathetic, but the food is to die for. And perhaps most importantly, you can tell your friends you ate there. You may put up with waiting weeks for a reservation, small portions, high cost and indifference. Could this be like a top 100, highly selective, brand name school?

Let's flip the scene here and go to a fast food place. When one goes to a Mickey D's, Wendy's, Arby's, Carl's, Burger King, Taco Bell, etc., you don't expect much service. A quick "May I take your order" and "Would you like to maxi-size yourself?" About it. But then, the customer does not have much invested in the place. Not like going to a multi-star place like the *French Laundry, La Bernadin, Gordon Ramsay, per se, or Charlie Trotter.* These are places where you must invest time waiting for the upcoming date of your reservation, spend time waiting to be seated, high expectations, and a great deal of money for small portions and squiggly gravy-like designs on the plate. At a fast food place, there is not much investment. Customers have low to moderate expectations for the service or product. This is not to say the customer may not enjoy what he or she buys at fast food outlets. People often like the food and the lack of anxiety over what it will be like this time. It will always be the same. The food is highly predictable, so we know exactly we'll get. A puck in a bun is a puck whether it is hamburger, chicken, fish or something yet to be defined fully in a bun, or outside the bun. Customers may well pay too much money for what they get, but that's okay. They have already calculated the investment and decided that it is acceptable. We don't expect much service at any of the fast food places. Low expectations, small investment of money and time leads to an easier acceptance of a lack of what one might normally consider service and an anticipated product. Expectations are fulfilled.

The same is true in colleges and universities. Expectations need to be filled. For example, students will put up with indifferent educational service from TA's who teach so they can work on their dissertation, underpaid adjuncts who need the job, apathetic faculty who care more about their research than student learning, yellowed note lectures and so on. They may also accept some disappointment from all of the above as well as rudeness, indifference to their individual concerns and learning, unresponsiveness to them as individuals with needs and integrity, if they will finally leave the college with a diploma that has the name of one of the 306 brand-name schools on it. The diploma with the name is the real service expected here. The name brand diploma certification lets everyone know the student graduated from an impressively ranked institution. But keep in mind that even the Harvards, Stanfords, Yales, Michigans, Dukes, etc. lose students because some students come to believe the end result, the product, is finally not worth it.

Just as the fanciest chef-named restaurants have people leave without eating after an excessive wait, or the food or service not meeting the full expectations, people and students will do all they can to overlook, accept or endure through weak teaching or food, rude waiters, faculty, staff and administrators to be able to say they dined or attended a prestigious name. Association has so much power after all. That's why people will spend large sums of money to buy jackets, sweatshirts or other items with the name of a famous school on them even if they have not graduated high school. If the are seen in the clothing, a positive and somewhat powerful association can be created in the eyes and minds of viewers.

Being seen in the right restaurant can endow a person with caché. Attending the right school can do the same. Some people will put up with whatever they have to so they can get in and stay at a name brand college or for that matter any university, college or career college. Some will not. It depends on what expectations they entered the school with and the value they place on the product they will receive from graduating.

Serve Customers When They Are Hungry

Want a positive response from students?

Easy: FILL THEIR BELLIES.

We have found that colleges are like fast food restaurants in the minds of students. They are places they go to learn when they are hungry for knowledge.

When they are hungry. These are the key words. Not when the restaurant feels like serving but when the customers are hungry.

Sure we older academic folk still adhere to notions of breakfast, lunch and dinner. But then we love traditions and traditional structure.

Not so the students we seek to recruit and retain. Breakfast. Not time for that. Lunch. Gotta run. I'll grab something. Family all gathered around the table for dinner. Ahhhhh, that Norman Rockwell picture will not be seen on Saturday Evening Post.com.

And the old burgers with the ketchup, mustard and pickle sitting wrapped under the warmer? Nope. I want it my way not the way it is easiest for your production line and workers. Won't do it my way? Someone else will, and I will go there. I will think beyond the bun.

Yet oddly enough the product is basically the same. The thin, high fat, low nutrition burger in a bun or ground up, seasoned in a taco shell.

Quality is not the issue as Mickey D found out a few years back when it tried to sell a low fat, more nutritional burger. Health? Certainly not. Just try to find a veggie burger even at Burger King which tried to launch them a few years back.

"When I want it" is the issue. Have you noticed yet how the fast food places have expanded their hours to serve those burgers and fries when the customer is hungry? Fourth meal anyone? Two a.m. at the take-out window? Ready when they want it.

Why? Because they like long, inconvenient hours for management and workers? No. Because that's when they want to eat. If restaurants want to sell burgers, they have to do so when the customer is hungry. Not simply when they feel they would like to serve.

Okay. A true example, observed a few months back while at a client college that is trying to increase its retention but will likely fail if it doesn't recognize the time needs of its client students

An adult student was talking to an advisor. Students could not register for courses without the okay of an advisor. The student explained, "My job is changing, and I need a tech writing course as soon as possible."

"No problem. We have an excellent one."

"Great. When can I start?"

"Well, let me see. The next semester starts in June."

"JUNE! No you don't understand. I need the course now. I need to take the course now. I need it for my new job. I can't wait until June."

"Well, I'm sorry but it's too late for this semester. June is the earliest. We had to cut back on sections because of financial issues," she said to his back as he walked out.

Where did he go? To another educational restaurant ten miles down the road that would serve him when he's hungry.

Would you stay in a restaurant that said it decided to not serve lunch today so come back later for dinner? No. You'd find somewhere else that'll serve you lunch now, when you are hungry. When you want it. And distance is not the question anymore as much as time is. If the commute is within 15 to 20 minutes, maybe up to half-an-hour, and the place has the course when I want to be there, give me the car keys.

An example. I taught in an executive MBA program that met all day, one weekend a month. Students drove over two hours to get there. Stayed overnight. Were in class all day. Gave up their weekends because the timing fit their schedule. It met their educational appetite.

Our campus customer audits have found college menus (i.e. course schedule and offerings) are not designed to meet student hunger at most schools. For instance, we offer the wrong courses at the wrong times. You can get an introductory appetizer in the fall in early morning but in the spring, the next course in the sequence is available for brunch and the student just has twenty minutes for lunch because other required course were scheduled in overlapping times. Or even worse, the first required course is offered in the fall but the second half of the required sequence is not even offered in the spring.

One thing we have realized is that if courses are not offered, students cannot sign up for them. And if they are hungry enough to learn and graduate, they will go elsewhere to get the course. Especially if that is the one course that they will need to graduate.

So what to do? Here are some suggestions.

Learn more about your students' educational eating habits. Find out when they may be hungry, rather than simply when you might wish to serve. And you may even wish to find how long they feel they want to feed as well. It may surprise you.

Stagger the start of some basic courses like English composition. They do not have to all start on the same day. Try offering a start every two weeks with varying time commitments and class lengths that match student hungry times.

Schedule to the customer. People want education when they need it and the hunger is there. Some colleges have realized this and schedule to need. They offer staggered starts throughout the semesters, condensed programs, variable formats, in class and online, fully digitized and hybrid. They are succeeding with their students, building market, enrollment and a reputation for great customer service that will lead to even greater success.

Study your offerings and schedule. See if you can provide students an educational menu with the right choices in the correct order for proper nutrition and pleasure. And oh yuh – do not substitute candy for real learning meat. Don't weaken content in an attempt to say you are meeting student needs.

To those who shake their heads and say, "Learning is not like fast food. It takes time to develop and maintain quality. Anything less than a semester length in normal times will lack integrity." Right! What about the three, four, five and six week summer courses we are offering to students to try to maintain some enrollment during the summer? If we can do it in the summer, why not all year round? And if the summer courses are not as good as regular semester courses why do we offer inferior education in the summer? Hypocrisy anyone?

Bottom line here is if you want a positive gut reaction, schedule offerings to meet the customer's hunger.

The Fiscal Power of Retention

The Investment to Expectations Relationship

The financial, emotion and personal investment in higher education is very high no matter what school a student attends. Students do choose schools by cost, by whether or not they can afford it. If a student cannot pay for tuition and fees, they cannot go, and they will attend a school they can better afford. Students will pay right up to what they can stretch to afford if they believe the school is worth the fiscal stretch. That actually makes all institutions scalable on fiscal and expectation levels by default.

It is important to keep in mind that there exists a cost value ratio for students and families as they consider applying to and staying in a college. There is a strong correspondence between the cost to attend, the need to sacrifice to meet the cost and the level of expectation for the school attended. The higher the cost, the greater the sacrifice, the more elevated the expectations.

That is not to say that students who attend a lower cost community college and may have much of the cost defrayed by Pell, for example, do not expect much from it. Not at all. Sacrifice is not only a money factor but an effect on lifestyle, time and effort consideration. For example, an adult student who has to find babysitting, adjust a work schedule around night classes and study into the late hours may well feel he is making a high level of investment to family and free time. As a result, students who may not struggle financially can still develop a set of very high expectations for attending school regardless of cost but based on their personal level of investment.

Every institution should strive to do all it can to assess and understand student investment factors and then do all it can to meet student expectations. It is both an ethical and practical responsibility. Ethical because the student places not only dollars in the school but the personal investment based on the institution's stated or implied promise to make the student's life better by attending the college. For instance, night students are often making a higher level personal sacrifice to attend than many day students for whom family finances are the more important investment.

The practical concerns are simple. If students feel – not understand but feel – their investment will not meet their expectations, they will drop out.

In most cases, the price-expectation ratio does not indicate a direct correlation of tuition cost to a student's ability to accept poor service and skeptical anticipation of an education, a degree and a job. Just because a student is given a scholarship or Pell Grant that covers some of the costs so their out-of-pocket is less does not lower their return on investment attitude. The only time the correlation of low price to expectation ratio may have force is when a student is on a full scholarship to a school he or she otherwise could not afford nor could the student afford other colleges of equal rank and prestige. The choices of these students can be limited, but the ratio can shift to the disadvantage of the school if the student had/has other scholarship options from another institution. Then the full scholarship student will adjust the ratio as would any other student, and if the investment is greater than the anticipated return, the full scholarship student may well exercise options.

Students will generally expect more education, training and service than they pay for whether they pay tuition and fees for a tier one school, a local public college or a non-ranked career college. It would be absolutely wrong for anyone to believe that since the school has low tuition costs students will accept less education or service for their lower payments. That would be like telling a student attending school on a scholarship he should be happy with whatever he gets and be uncomplainingly grateful. "Hey, you get what you pay for, and you didn't pay anything." I don't think that approach will work. Or for that matter, exorbitantly high tuition does not guarantee either a great education, famous professors teaching or excellent customer service though the learning is more likely at some quite expensive schools, as actually it can be at less expensive schools. Learning can and does take place even better than at the name brand university at many less expensive but student-focused institutions.

The Difficulty to Pay to Expectation Ratio

There is also a very important relationship between the difficulty and/or the struggle to pay for school and the expectations of a first generation college family. If the student is the first to attend college in the family, two opposing forces come into play. Some families will place no or little value on college attendance. No one has gone to college. College is for others in society but not for them. Education may also be seen as a threat to the family and its culture since a college diploma might set up divisions between family, community and the graduate. College can even be seen as taking on airs and trying to be better than others who reject education. Moreover, the families and community see themselves as working class and the faster to the job and paycheck the better. College is an interruption in the flow.

Students from these families and backgrounds are always at risk for dropping out if they do not perceive or receive their personal vision of learning and expected outcome. They are most always struggling to pay for school, often cannot get loans because no one will cosign a loan, may get Pell but it often does not make up some of the living costs for them since there is no family support. They are also struggling against social pressures that can become very overpowering. As a result, their expectations can become very high and difficult to obtain especially if they may have had an inadequate K-12 preparation.

The other scenario is when the family realizes the importance of a college education and ends up placing an immense pressure on the student and the cultural images of college. If the student and/or family struggles to pay for college, there is a strong demand for services such as extra help, counseling and intervention as well as a result that is more or less in direct correlation to the difficulty of paying. If a family has to give up dining in four star restaurants and make do with three stars to pay the bills, well that's one thing. But if the family has to give up lunches or heating to pay…

Struggle increases the demand pressures in the investment-expectation ratio. Don't ever tell a single mother who is scrimping on everything to pay for a degree that she is privileged to be able to attend college. Or that she should be happy she got into the class even if she finds it boring, useless and the professor is not all that understanding of her coming in late because the babysitter was late. And yes, you and I have heard these statements and even worse.

Students and those paying the education carry the conviction and corresponding demand that attending and graduating from a school will lead to the desired product – a diploma and a job. No school is given a slide on meeting those expectations. But it has to be accepted that the 306 name brands do get a bit more leeway since a major part of the product they offer is their name on the diploma as the expected key to a good career. The imprimatur is considered so valuable that people will accept a weaker educational and service product if they come to gain the name recognition. Sort of like the folks who camped out on sidewalks and suffered accompanying deprivations (some even more than one night) to get the I-phone the day they came out, so they could say they have one of the first ones.

A Price More Precious than Rubies

Though tuition, fees, books, food, transportation and other costs can be major obstacles and concerns for many people, these are not the only significant investments in higher education a student will make. The true cost is in a belief and a placement of trust that the college will care about me as a person and student. That it will do all it can to help me succeed. And, that the career school, college or university will supply the real services of helping me graduate and get a job, or into grad school.

The investment here is in no way comparable to a meal that may be great but will soon be gone and forgotten. Nor a flat puck that I eat on the run to keep from being hungry. It is not in buying anything material at all. The investment is in a dream, an aspiration that the buyer expects will be realized by attending a particular school. The investment is in my future. In my life. In ME. The meal I wish to be served and eat in higher education is the knowledge, the training and the preparation for my success. The services I expect and demand are the ones that will help me get to that table of life as they grow my sense of value, worth and integrity.

In most every case and school, students will not want to be mistreated along the way. They will not accept having their dream blurred or erased. Students will not tolerate having the instructional services and assistance they need to succeed not being available or taken away. If they believe they need help, it had better be made available, or the trust the student brought into the relationship will erode – even at a brand name school. In fact, we found that students who leave a college most often leave for customer service reasons. But that reason may not simply be that people at the school trained at Durgin Park.

It's not simply the action, the smiling and the service performance of a person like a waitress or an administrator in isolation from the result, the product that determines what good service is. It is a more complex interaction of expectation, investment, process, actions and, certainly, outcome or final result. Courtesy, smiling, helping and attention to wants are services expected and will definitely help with retention. They are core aspects of customer service after all. A fun college experience with nice people is certainly important and if it is missing from a university, it can and will lose students. But the experience is not the only determinate.

The final and most important service a college or university can and must provide is *keeping the faith.* Meeting the trust that everything a student goes through, pays for and learns will help lead to the objective of getting a job or into graduate school is the key trust the student embeds into attendance.

And just as a believer in a faith needs counseling at times when something occurs to possibly challenge the faith, so students need counseling – academic, occupational, financial and perhaps even personal – to be able to maintain their faith. If a school does not provide at least on-demand academic, occupational and financial services in these areas, it is opening itself to a crack, a fracturing in the faith. Not having important services available to students such as counseling will lead to at least micro-fractures in the students' confidence and trust in the school. As we have learned from Henry Petroski in his excellent 1992 book *To Engineer Is Human: The Role of Failure in Successful Design*, micro-fractures grow into larger fissures that sooner or later allow airplane wings to fall off and bridges to fall down. In the area of retention, wings may not fall off but the funds from students dropping out can seriously hurt the institution's ability to fly.

The Fiscal Power of Retention

There was a time during orientation at college when an administrator, often the president, would tell the new beanie-wearing freshman, "Look to the right of you. Then look to the left of you. One of you will not be here by the end of the year." That statement was intended to frighten students into being serious in their studies and re-assert the toughness of the academic program at the school. Higher education was still considered a privilege not a right, even though the GI Bill, then Korea, and community colleges were radically changing that situation. The belief was not everyone was *college material* and it was the school's job to sort of those with the *right stuff* from those who were made of lesser substance. That was the self-perceived role of higher education. Separate the wheat from the chaff, if you will. Retention was not an issue to be concerned with at all.

But the world has certainly changed. There are many more schools now. The proprietary sector has gone from cosmetology and truck driving to PhD's. Correspondence schools on match books have become omnipresent, study anywhere, anytime online, enrolling machines. Competition for students is intense and admission departments are feeling the stress as are the budgets of colleges, universities and career schools that have had to make difficult decisions to balance the budget when they do not *make their numbers.*

And yet, not enough of higher education has really adapted to the changes. It is still *admissions, admissions and again admissions.* Bring in more and more new bodies, or as one overly pragmatic administrator is alleged to have said at the University of Phoenix, "Get asses in the classes. That's the goal." And it is certain that though this person may have been caught saying that hundreds of others simply were not reported when they also made that or a similar statement. Recruitment and admissions is still seen as *the* key to the major aspect of operating revenue. I recall quite well the proclamation of the CEO of one of the large career college groups. "There isn't a problem that exists that can't be fixed by enrolling more students." He was speaking not just for his proprietary group but for most every not-for-profit, for-profits, public and private college and university in the country.

The on-going and most frequent discussions in campus business meetings and with trustees still focus on the question, "What's our budget target? How many did we admit? How many have committed to the next freshman class? How many have put down their deposits? How many do we figure will actually show?" *Strategic* enrollment and revenue planning tend to be summed up with, "We may have a budget problem for next year? Increase tuition and enroll more students!" This has become the annual approach at most colleges and universities.

And when schools lose students during the school year the questioning starts with, "What did we budget for attrition?" That is followed by the response, "It's okay. We planned for 34% drops in the budget. As long as we don't lose more than we budgeted for we'll be okay."

That is a dumb business model. Of course any business, including higher education, has to figure in customer/client defection and loss of market share. But planning to lose upwards of a third of all their customers and all the costs associated with acquiring them each and every year is a confident way of making sure the institution is always running a tight budget. A self-fulfilling profligacy if you will.

A key factor to retaining and growing revenue and operating success is not in admitting students, but in keeping them. It can be understood that in the days of "look left and right" retaining too many students might be considered a sign of a weak academic program. It was also a time of much smaller operating costs and budgets. Presidential salaries were not in the up-to-a-million-dollars level. Faculty lived on the love of learning and free summers. Health costs were affordable and so on. Who talked about retention as an important aspect of a college? But today, in the world of ever-increasing salaries, health costs, debt service, fixed costs, technology and equipment acquisition alongside decreasing public support, and an extremely competitive enrollment market, how can people not think of retention? Yet, they manage not to.

Retention is where the real revenue is created. Admissions costs money – significant amounts of money. Retaining students/clients costs from nothing to very little. Retaining students through graduation is also how colleges, universities and career schools meet their higher calling, their missions, their purpose and reason to exist and be supported. Students and learning are still the key publicly conceived rationale for higher education. Granted the old saying is still out there, "This would be a great place to work if it weren't for the students." But without the students, undergraduates primarily, there would be no place to work. Society supports higher education because it believes college prepares students for the economy, for society and for life.

It is important for schools to make the shift now from an admissions concentration to an admissions AND retention focus; from churn and burn to learn and earn. From keep them coming in and if they leave replace them to admit and work with students so they succeed in their endeavors. A more balanced learn and earn approach will also allow the college to retain the revenues it needs to succeed, meet the mission and grow.

The Hierarchy of Student Decision-Making

Over the past years, we have been interviewing students to listen and better understand what they seek from going to college. We also sought to hear what motivates them to make their decisions to choose a school or leave it.

There is much we learned from the 618 students each year. One of the things we came to understand is that there is a five step hierarchy of student concerns that guides most of their decision-making in choosing a school and deciding to stay or leave. These steps in the hierarchy are governed primarily by some logical decision-making. The emotional aspects of fit and all seemed to be there but it did not come up except as a last aspect of the decision hierarchy when the other four preceding, or more important steps were answered in their minds.

The hierarchy takes the form of five questions students (and parents) think about when considering a college, university or career school to attend. Can I get in? Can I afford it? Can I graduate? Can I get a job? And Will I like it?

In some ways the questions parallel the organization of Maslow's Hierarchy of Need which starts at physiological concerns such as breathing, eating, drinking, procreating – all issues that are basic to just staying alive. Also as with Maslow, simply because a question or need is fulfilled at a point in time does not mean a student will not regress down the hierarchy to return to a lower-level need. This will almost always occur for example when tuition, fees, housing, meal tickets and so on come due for payment. The need to focus on the question "Can I afford it?" comes back until the question is answered.

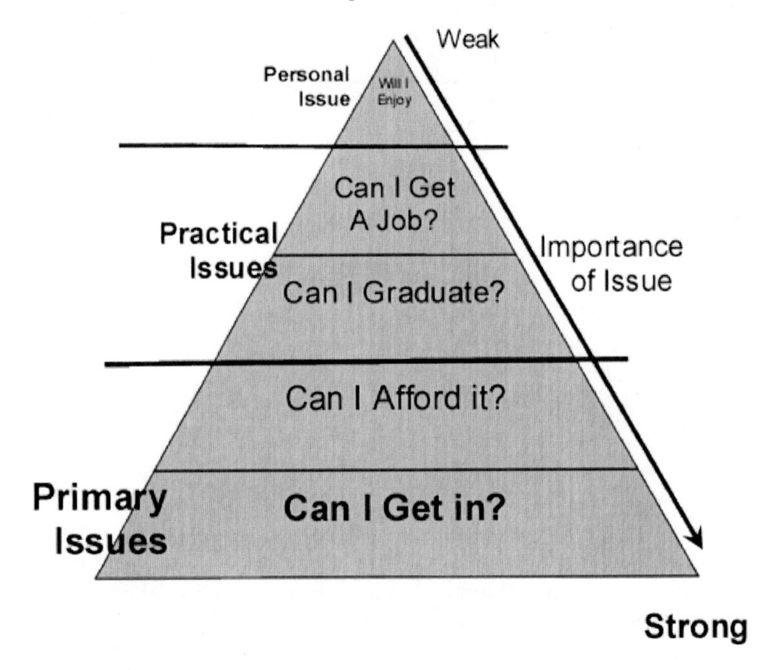

The Taxonomy of Student Decision - Making

ACADEMICMAPS

In Maslow's Hierarchy which starts at the basic level of physiological needs required for life, without being alive, none of the following higher level needs matter after all. If one is dead, it is hard to worry about anything else. And so it is with the Student Decision Hierarchy. They proceed from basic issues of being alive in a decision process such as getting accepted to the school. They then move from lower/basic considerations of necessity and immediacy to considerations of return on investment (ROI), the future and even the issue of satisfaction. But the question of a satisfying experience is the last issue for consideration by students. This placement suggests a parallel to Maslow's category of esteem but maybe not yet self-actualization. Enjoying school can only be a concern after the very practical survival issues from gaining entrance to a job are addressed. Having the basic and practical considerations resolved allows a student to worry about having a good time as a decision point.

So what does this say to us?

It says that students start from basic and practical considerations toward their college experience as a means to an end. Granted, not every single one perhaps. There are students who may go to college for the parties and the college experience or because their parents have told them they will go. Students in these groups may not deal with the issues of the hierarchy seriously, but then they are usually not serious students and have a tendency to either do something academics refer to as *flunk out* or eventually get with the script. Those that are going to flunk out because they really do not attend the college except to participate in its social life are seldom students we can affect positively no matter what we do. So we cannot focus too much effort on them but on the major cohorts of students who can be affected positively to stay at the school through customer service.

To do so, a significant part of customer service needs to focus on their hierarchical concerns and how they see college. They see it, as we already know from the annual CIRP UCLA Freshman Attitudes study, as a means to an end, a job/career. For students, that end is quite practical just as the hierarchy shows the beginning decision-making is. At their core, students are practical about attending higher education. From start to finish, students go to college and will stay at a school if it can supply that objective of a job.

Sure they would like to enjoy the experience but they will endure it if that means they can get that job. That is the major focus They wish to enjoy their time at college, but they cannot do that until we serve their other more pressing concerns – paying for it, getting what they need to graduate and finally, an assurance they can get a job or get into a good grad school on the way to a career from their college experience.

Although students are practical and career-focused in the drive to attend and stay at a school, what we find is that most schools spend most of their time, money and effort attempting to affect the highest-level, lowest need concern in the hierarchy – enjoying school. From the first day of orientation, "You'll love it here." is the focus when perhaps focusing more on paying for school in the future, graduation and careers is a better investment. It may be that when we concentrate too much on trying to make students enjoy their experience, we are not serving them as well as we could. Nor are we necessarily helping retention as we will discuss in the next section which continues the discussion on the Hierarchy of Student Decision-Making.

Hierarchy Step 1: Can I Get In?

The first issue, **Can I Get In?,** is of course the most primary and pragmatic of the concerns. After all, if a student can't gain acceptance to a school, all the other issues are moot. If they cannot be admitted, they never have to worry at all about whether they can pay for it or if they will be able to graduate from the school. Not being admitted negates the other situations. Therefore, students put the most effort into choosing schools they believe they can gain entry into.

This does not mean they do not attempt to get into schools which they know are long shots, because if they do somehow get into a *selective college* they have still answered the question. In fact, if they are accepted into a school that was a stretch they feel better about their initial acceptance.

They are also immediately thrown into an at-risk situation because they may believe they could be able to succeed and graduate, but the school may actually be less sure. Too many schools accept students who are marginal so they can assure they have the *right* number of students to start the year and revenue stream. These schools may partially delude themselves into believing they are providing a chance to the student, but too very often the acceptance is to meet less altruistic goals. Keep in mind that colleges build what they believe may be the annual attrition percentage into the budget. If it is planned for, then that is an acceptable attrition number. It may not be as acceptable to the students who either fail or decide that this college was not for them. But let's keep in mind the budgetary needs of the school even if they could not be compatible with the financial condition of a marginal student.

As you might have guessed from the minor irony above, not only is selling the wrong school to the wrong student poor customer service, it is ethically challenged. Admitting students who really are marginal is neither fair to the students nor the school. Clearly the students who are accepted into the wrong school and drop out because of bad fit are cheated. The have wasted money, time and more importantly, a large part of their self-confidence and emotional investment.

The school also loses. Sure, it loses money, but it also is cheated out of its ability to fulfill a section of its mission. It has defaulted on its chance to improve someone's life and future. The college has lost the ability to make a difference in the future not just of a person but the society and culture.

So, perhaps schools should be certain that they use a variation of the primary question to assure they provide appropriate customer service to its students and itself, and that question that should be answered honestly.

Should this student get in to begin with?

Is an enrollment that important? Should it be?

Keep in mind that a rather steady and strongly correct argument I have been making is that retention has power. Retain more students and the admission numbers can actually become less important. Retention reduces the need to replace drops, which is a major factor in admission's quotas. Simply put, if admissions does not have to replace as many emptied slots, they and the school require fewer new students to come in.

Hierarchy Step 2: Can I Afford It?

Once the primary concern of getting in is satisfied, an immediate issue comes flying forward. Can I pay for this? Though it will seem at times that some students give the impression that college should be free just like high school was, most will realize that it costs money to go to school. As to whether or not college should be free or at least affordable for most students is an issue for another day.

Very often students who are looking to go to a school concentrate so much on hierarchy question one, Can I Get In?, that they put off worrying about paying. Students will actually not encounter the reality of paying for college until they are admitted and are sent a bill. They will have an idea of costs since most will have looked at schools by some sense of cost banding.

Cost bands

A cost band is a mental grouping by tuition such as high, medium and low costs schools in relation to the student's or the family's self-conceived economic position and social connections. For example, students from an affluent neighborhood may assume that any of the top Name Brand schools will be affordable because they live in an affluent area and everyone else seems to be applying to Ivies or name brands. So they apply to schools in an expensive but affordable cost band that others would see as way out of their reach. A student from the inner city would not see her band including the expensive private schools for the most part. A student from a solidly middle class neighborhood or town would look to schools that fit within the affordability band appropriate to the family's income. They might apply to state universities and colleges as well as a *stretch school* which expands the band itself with the hope that "If I get in, we can find a way to pay for it." In fact, banding is a bit elastic since students are pushed to apply for a stretch school and worry about the costs later. Moreover, many students do not consider the real costs as they apply.

The banding often expands beyond the financial means for many families due to a couple of elasticity factors. First is the culturally promoted belief that anyone can become president, and there is a way to pay for every student to attend the college or university of his or her choice. Anyone who has had to pay for school knows this is a cultural fabrication that is only true for those with the discretionary income to pay or the credit rating to take out loans that will lower the family's fiscal stability and/or the student's life after graduation for years to come. And the becoming president part? It's true that C students have done it but there was that family money and connections thing.

The second band elasticity factor is set upon another misbelief often promoted by the school itself which talks vaguely about scholarships and grants available for those who qualify. As part of the recruitment approach, costs are left out of the discussion or details. "Oh tuition is $X but most of our students get scholarships and grants to help out" is a quite common line many admission reps will repeat to answer the tuition affordability question. Scholarships and grants do exist but not in the amount or quantity required by most students to be able to afford the school of their choice. Scholarships and grants such as Pell can help out, but many students who elect to go to a school that is really outside of their fiscal band will be left with large debts.

At the same time, there is a psychological factor that restricts band elasticity from including what might be sensible and feasible financial decisions. This is the socially acceptable aspect of choices that dictate the range of schools that may be included in the band. For example, students from an affluent area would not place a community college into their band since that would carry too high a social esteem cost. The affective return on investment would be far too low. To even be known as considering a community college (which is a very wise fiscal choice for the first two years by the way) would lower the social status. So the banding is a combination of perceived financial and social cost.

The initial selection of schools to apply to might have some fiscal controls on it but once the applications go out, the *can I get in* stage takes full command. Actual costs remain secondary to gaining acceptance. During this stage, hope springs eternal and the *first get in and then we'll figure it out* attitude is prevalent until acceptance. When the letter comes welcoming a student to the school, then issue 2 takes complete importance. Reality suddenly comes in the door with the welcoming package. What often doesn't come with the package is enough help and customer service assistance with financial aid.

Making Financial Aid Even More Difficult

Yes, most schools send out some details about financial aid and what the family must do, but the information usually confuses the potential student and parents. It is almost always written in academic in-group language as well as the state and federal legalese to make sure the students and parents do not really understand what they need to do and then how to do it. There are times when I have this cynical belief that we use confusing and technical language to dissuade families from applying for all the financial aid they might be entitled to. This cynicism is not all that far-fetched either. The June 2007 *Harvard Business Review* has an article by Gail McGovern and Youngme Moon. The article's title is *Companies and the Customer Who Hate Them.* The article discusses companies that deliberately confuse customers into making bad purchases.

Companies have found that confused and ill-informed customers, who often end up making poor purchasing decisions, can be highly profitable indeed (p. 79)… the majority of firms have unwittingly fallen into a trap. Without ever making a deliberate decision to do so, they have, over a period of years taken greater advantage of their customers. (p.80)

And when schools make it even more difficult than it needs to be to properly complete financial aid requests and applications for scholarships or grants, they are doing what McGovern and Moon found companies doing. It seems as if there has developed a probably unconscious yet insidious lack of real help that frustrates, confuses and stupefies parents and students trying to complete the required forms. As colleges and universities tried to follow state and federal rules they found Byzantine and impervious to full understanding without seminars on them, they have simply repeated them verbatim to parents. Most all of them do not know what to do really. Want to see if it is true for your school? Just open your catalog and read what's there. Then look at the financial aid information sent to parents. Does your information provide your customers the service they need? Likely not. It includes such helpful directions as "COMPLETE THE FAFSA ONLINE. Don't forget to enter your pin!" Bowling or brooch?

To most people these three words are tantamount to, "Here is your do-it-yourself proctoscope kit". I have never found anyone who found completing the FAFSA easy or enjoyable even if they knew what they were doing. They remind parents and students of the joy of doing their annual taxes. What school would not want to be considered in the same thought as the IRS?

Parents hate the forms whether they are online or not. Colleges should realize this and provide them all the human help they can. Briarcliffe College in New York does this by having people come to the school and sit through a full introduction to the FAFSA online. Then if the people bring their materials in, Tuition Planners help them complete the forms so they can get every penny for which they qualify. I even observed a planner helping a father whose other son was going to a different school complete the forms for the other school. I believe I heard that the father was talking to the other son about transferring to the college that provided real service for students – service that made financial aid easier and more profitable for everyone. The students have more money to make college more affordable, and the school has greater assurance of the student being able to pay and attend.

I am amazed at how many parents and students do all they can to not complete the FAFSA, either online or in hardcopy. All they need is one excuse not to complete it and they will leave it for later or just never get it done. For instance, I have discovered over the years that there is one bit of information that too often provides parents a perfect excuse not to complete the FAFSA and send it in. And that one bit of information is one that you should make sure is right there for them because it affects you directly. It is the college code number. For some reason, we hide these numbers from students and their families.

Try this, go to your financial aid office and see if the code is posted in an unobstructed, easily noticeable location, or in a somewhat prominent spot or for that matter, anywhere. Odds are pretty good it is not. Yet, without that code, students cannot complete their FAFSA, and if they cannot or do not complete it, who is ultimately hurt? Sure the student, but the school too. Without the financial aid the student might get, he or she is not coming there. All the time, effort and money spent to recruit that student is just lost, as is the chance to provide that student the best education he or she could get anywhere. The faculty loses the chance to fulfill its mission to educate that student.

So get the college code out there. Post it in the office. Print it on the forms. Make sure it can be obtained easily on the financial aid section of the website. Also, help people with the form. Provide counselors who actually call potential students to offer their aid in completing the form. Create an online tutorial for parents to use as they complete the form. Offer hybrid workshops that will take a group of parents from the start of the form through to the end. Hybrid? Online and by conference call. Also, provide them at the school. Invite parents in to complete their forms with hands-on assistance.

Ways to Make It Affordable

Make sure you help students and their families answer the question, Can I afford it? If they do not believe they can, they won't, EVEN IF THEY ACTUALLY COULD.

Do you have a payment plan? A way for normal people to make payments for school over a period of time? Most people get paid weekly, bi-weekly or even monthly, yet we want it all at one time. Lump sum. No other major investment people make calls for all the money up front. A house – a mortgage. A car – five year loan. Even a doctor's bill can be charged and paid out over time. College? Not always so.

The hardest thing for people to do in paying a college is to save it all up to make a single payment. Life often gets in the way. Yet, if they can plan for regular payments, college can be affordable. Provide a payment plan that allows them to be able to pay for school over a semester or year or even longer if possible. There are many ways to do this. Twenty percent down and then monthly payments. Run an in-house plan or let a professional do it for you. Charge for the service or not. There are many ways to do it, but do it.

If you cannot make college affordable or at least within reach of affordability, students cannot answer the step 2 question, Can I afford it?, and will not come to school. Or if they do start they will soon run out of money and drop out. In fact this is the major reason why there are fiscal drops in the second semester and sophomore years.

Hierarchy Step 3: Can I Graduate?

Though it might strike some as odd, students attend college not to learn as a primary goal, but to graduate. They are in school to obtain the certification needed to obtain their entry into a career. The first step on that path to a job and a better life is graduation.

If a student starts to believe that he or she may not be able to graduate for any reason, that student is surely starting a movement to the door marked exit. So colleges should do all they can to ethically assist students to graduate.

By the way, when you think about it, we all went to college to graduate. That's why we took the required course and grumbled about them. That is why as an English major I read and studied the Romantic poets. It was a requirement for me to be able to get the degree. If I could have avoided Wordsworth, I would have. Though it may be rather Wal-Martish of me to admit it, I tend to enjoy Lucy in Peanuts over Wordsworth's. And my reading of the stanza goes like this:

> What fond and wayward thoughts will slide
> Into a student's head!
> 'O mercy!' to myself I cried,
> 'I could not care if Lucy turned up dead.'

But if I wanted to graduate I had to not only study but also pretend that I liked Wordsworst's Lucy, since I knew the professor did. I did so to pass the course and graduate. Just as you and every other student did.

Graduation Is the Goal

The goal was and is graduation. And if there is anything placed in a student's path that will keep them from graduating, they will either find a way, go elsewhere or just plain drop out. The third is the more popular decision it seems since the numbers from the National Center for Educational Statistics' 2006 report indicates that of the cohort of new students entering baccalaureate degree programs in 1998, 35% obtained a degree in four years and 54% completed within six years. In community colleges, just 33% of those who started in 2001 have graduated (NCES, 2007-154).

Table 6. *Graduation rates of bachelor's-seeking students at 4-year Title IV institutions, by control of institution, gender, and time to degree: United States, cohort year 1999*

	All	Public	Private	For-Profit
4-year graduation rate (%)	35.3	27.9	50.2	22.1
5-year graduation rate (%)	52.3	48.3	61.0	26.9
6-year graduation rate (%)	57.1	54.1	64.0	29.1

(NCES 2007-154 p. 12)

And yes, the argument goes that it is difficult to establish *correct* and *acceptable* graduation rates as well as expected rates in four, five and six years, because students vary so much. Some take longer than 6 years. That's their choice. Some only go for a year, which was their goal. And actually, graduation should not be the accountability point because even if a student drops out before graduation, higher education has provided some added value that would not have been there if the school did not provide an opportunity, etc., etc. We all know these are rationalizations to stave off the cognitive dissonance created by allowing students to start at a school when we know they may not be able to graduate. "But who are we to deny the opportunity"...to gain another tuition?

Actually colleges and universities have a higher ethical obligation to the students. They should not admit those who likely will not succeed at that university or college. But for those they do admit, the institution must accept its ethical obligation to do all it can to assist the students to graduate. By admitting a student the school is saying you can do it, and we are certifying that with acceptance. "You may be from a very weak high school, may not have enough money to buy books and eat and may not fit into our campus culture but come on in. We believe in you and your possibility, slim though we know it may be, to graduate." That admission represents what should be a shared commitment to the student's success. If the student is willing and does all he or she can to succeed, the school should feel obligated to do all it can to help that student graduate. The university should provide all the developmental assistance students may need. There should be professional tutoring available to help students succeed in every class we have them take. If professional counseling, either academic or personal is called for, that should be available. If we know (and we do) that students do not come to college with the study skills needed to succeed, teach them study skills. If they have never really had to worry about their financial situation, teach them money management skills. If they do not know how to manage their time and come to classes sleep deprived because of it; teach them time management. These are some true customer services.

If we accept them, we should be ready to provide all the help and service they need to succeed. If we do not, we may well be entering the red zone of ethical behavior.

The student is coming to college to graduate after all; not just get seats to home football games and wear a school sweatshirt. The student is endowing the institution with trust and faith that it will help the student get to his or her life and career goals. And again, achieving those goals depends on graduating. And don't hand me Michael Dell or Bill Gates unless you wish to argue that maybe higher education is not needed by exceptional individuals who were destined to be millionaires without our brilliant teaching.

We cannot really worry about some students who will leave because they realize that they cannot pass a required course or the foreign language requirement or calculus or whatever the faculty have set as required courses at the university. If the institution has established a set of core requirements that it considers as necessary to a valid education, and a student cannot complete them due to his or her inability even when help is provided, the institution almost has no choice but to either dismiss the student or let the student leave. It should not lower its standards or requirements just to keep students enrolled. That would be unethical.

Yes, the student wants to graduate, but if he or she is not capable of performing at a required level, it is not good customer service to just pass the student on to make him or her feel good. Moreover, the kindness of a sympathy pass will likely catch up to the student at some time. So, though the nursing department causes complaints when the student's final grade is a 69.4 and a 70 is required to move on and they won't give the extra .6 points so Tiffany or Rodney can graduate, the department is right. Supporting those standards is important. Customer service is not passing a nursing student on so he or she might harm someone later in life.

Learn and Earn

For most schools, life is a treadmill. Just keep running and lose calories? Not quite. More of churn admissions and burn enrollments. That's our basic MO, and it is a losing one. Loss of students does equal loss of revenue, loss of morale, loss of integrity and loss of the chance to actually meet that mission statement so prominent in catalogs but not many other places I fear. Churn and burn is a loss not just for students but for schools.

It is demoralizing for everyone not just to have to constantly work to attract and serve larger numbers of news students. It is even more demoralizing to see the students everyone worked hard to recruit, enroll and integrate into the school walk out the back door at astoundingly high rates. This situation is very common at most colleges and universities today. The only ones who escape some of it are the brand name schools that do attract a more fully committed and often more capable, wealthier, traditional student. But then, they are putting their resources into supporting a fairly unified student body of traditional full-time 18- to 24-year-old student straight from high school. Many schools do not have that luxury. Their student bodies are very heterogeneous. These are often the students who are not the *better* students. They are students who bring their hopes, dreams and needs along with them.

This is especially true of *neo-traditional students*. Those students who used to be called non-traditional (adults, single parents, minorities, lower socio-economic students) who have become sought after enrollment prospects for schools to make their admission quotas. The neo-traditionals know that their cohorts graduate at much lower rates than the traditionals who came from better schools, families with an educational focus and money to at least obtain loans and be able to pay them off.

The March 23, 2007 *Chronicle of Higher Education* article "The Graduation Gap" states:

> ...students from low-income backgrounds are less likely to graduate from college than their wealthier peers. For college students from families with annual incomes of $25,000 or less, slightly one in four earns a bachelor's degree within six years...For students from families with annual incomes of $70,000 or more, that figure is 57% percent.

One in four. Wonder if students in the lower income cohorts are concerned about their own chance to be in that 25%? You bet they are. And they worry whether you and your college also worry enough to do all that can be done to get them into the 25% rather than just labeling them as not better students and setting in place the self-fulfilling prophecy that these were really not college material anyhow.

And the 57% from better economic backgrounds? Wonder if they.... Hey wait a minute! Only 57%. That means 43% of all students who start higher education do not get a degree? Do not graduate in six years? Sure some take longer but this means that a huge number of students just do not graduate. They do not graduate! Not from your school. Not from any school or university.

But do not believe I will argue for every school trying to recruit *better* students. My argument goes to how we can make the students we do recruit the best they can be. Not to degrade the student body by letting the students know they are not as valued as those students who get into and attend the so-called top schools.

With those numbers in mind, do you start to see why hierarchical question number 3 – "Can I graduate?" – remains a very important and ever present concern? These numbers should help make clear that since graduation and the degree is why people attend and pay for college, students will quit or at least transfer to another school where they feel they may have a better chance to graduate.

If students do not believe a college will help them answer their taxonomic question 3, it will lose them. If a college does not help students answer the question and then help them graduate, that is a sure way to increase attrition through dropouts and transfers.

But it is not just a fiscal consideration for institutions of higher learning to assist the students they admit, it is an ethical responsibility. When a college accepts a student and takes his or her money that forms a contract. It is not a contract for good grades but for the services needed to assist the client in being successful in his or her college career and that means graduate. That is what students are at a college for. To graduate. Yes, there are some who just come to attend a class or two and if that is their real objective, fine, but for the preponderance of students, graduation and a career are the goals. To finally graduate is why they applied, paid their money to enforce the contract and are attending.

Included in that contract has to be a belief that every student that is accepted into the college is capable of succeeding and making it to graduation. If a college or university were to accept students and their money but not believe they could succeed, that would not just be excessively unethical, it is almost criminal fraud. Fraud unless the school is prepared to provide the assistance that may be needed to complete the contract successfully by both parties. The school should – must – know if students it admits may need assistance to be able to succeed in all areas of study. So they must also realize that they will need to help the students with those needs. They should not be able to step back and just act as if "Okay, you are accepted into the college, now you are on your own. Sink or swim."

Sink or swim is not a good retention or customer service position. Drownings never make for good image or reputation. Helping them swim is a much better way to go for you and for them.

Focus on Helping Them Succeed

We must focus on helping students succeed – not just in freshman year remedial courses but with help, assistance and attention to their needs every year, every week and every day. They ask the question about staying in classes and staying in the school over and over again. Some every week; some every day. Be there to help students answer the question with academic and service assistance, with tutoring services that are important enough to make sure tutors know enough to really tutor. An ill-equipped or pedagogically weak tutor is not a help to anyone.

I have a bet for anyone reading this. You name the stake. Here is the bet. I wager your school does not care enough about students graduating to either have enough tutors or to ever train them in how to tutor, to teach. If you do, let me hear about it. Consider also that most schools use *peer* tutors – a euphemism that means we use the cheapest labor we can find even if they may not know all that much more than the people they try to help. Peer tutors are other students, often from the same class! They may be bright enough in class but not smart enough to be able to find ways to explain and help the student in need. I mean let's face it, we have enough people with Ph D's in front of classes who do not know how to teach, and they do have more education. Plus they have experienced more teaching so perhaps by some form of amoeba-like osmosis they picked up some techniques. But, why believe an under-educated peer/student with no teaching ability or training can do the trick for the weakest students?

If tutoring is supposed to help retain students by supplying help to make them believe they can succeed, at least train the tutors. Give the students and the tutors a chance to be successful. Correspondingly, get some classroom professionals to do the tutoring and drop the peer idea. A rather small investment in professional tutors can reap very large revenue savings. One tutor at say $30,000 plus benefits who helps keep 20 students in school at 20 X tuition...You do the math.

Customer Service-Based Scheduling

A bottom line customer service objective of the college should at least be to avoid throwing unnecessary roadblocks in the way of graduation. Yet basic institutional systems and *that's how we do it* concepts are set in place to make sure graduation may be tough to obtain. And certainly difficult in the two or four-year plan. Scheduling, for example.

Most every college or university president is more concerned with happy faculty than happy students. That's because faculty have a unique ability to make life miserable and even get a president fired. Complaints, committees, grievances, votes of no confidence tend to make presidents and other senior administrators anxious since trustees are bothered by them. Students, they know, will complain but since they generally fear retribution or feel powerless, they usually go away. They seldom go to the Board or if they do, many Boards do not have a procedure to hear them. Put simply, unhappy students seldom cause a college real angst or job loss except when the revenue drops into deficit because they drop out or do not enroll to start with.

The same follows for the basics of scheduling courses. The process is most normally done at the department level where the department chair certainly wishes to keep the full-time faculty happy, or they might turn on him or her. *I could lose their support and the chair. That would mean having to teach again. And my God, teaching a fuller load! No, it is better to keep the faculty happy.* So the chair finds out when and what the faculty want to teach. Oddly enough, most full-time faculty prefer not to teach required under-graduate courses or at inconvenient hours or four days a week. (Forget five. Most colleges and universities have stopped scheduling

Friday altogether.) Given the choice, faculty would want to teach something that interests them as an elective whether or not the subject fits students' graduation needs or schedules. In fact, at many schools, there are more elective sections taught in a semester or term than required course sections.

Scheduling should actually focus on student needs first and last. Required courses and sections should be scheduled first and at times that are best for students to attend. Times that will facilitate their attending, learning and progress toward graduation. And it might be Friday morning. Next, courses required for graduation within a particular major should be scheduled. Following these, any and all sequential courses that have already begun should be scheduled. For example, if students started French 1 last semester make sure French 2 is offered in the current semester and 3 will be available next. To be sure there will be a large enough class in French 3, figure out the attrition sequence and get a large enough French 1 class to meet the number goals of French 3. After these are scheduled, the non-required electives that faculty feel like teaching because they'd make them happy to do so can be scheduled in remaining slots. That is an example of good customer service and helping students answer the *can I graduate* question to assure increased retention.

Figuring the Real Cost of Sections

Since budgets have been cut, fewer sections are offered period. Colleges and universities just cut back on the number of course sections offered and then cull out sections with small numbers to save on the budget. For some reason, perhaps academic tradition, colleges and universities often use the number 10 as the required number of students enrolled to let a class go forward. That in itself befuddles fiscal reality.

Consider that the average number of adjuncts teaching course sections in the average college or university has risen to somewhere between 50% and 64% and could be more if figured by individual departments. That's the number of adjuncts by the way, not the percentage of courses taught by them. That number is not available but could run as high as 75% considering full-time teaching loads, reductions in loads and such. And though I have only anecdotal information, it seems most of the introductory courses and required courses not taught by the newly hired full-time faculty are taught either by adjuncts or TA's who are often part-time grad students. So the odds are quite good that a course section, especially required or introductory courses, will be taught by a low pay adjunct or T.A.

All the above is to question whether or not students are receiving the most important customer service of good teachers who are dedicated to their learning and available to assist them when they need help. Maybe not. But what the numbers show is that most courses in colleges and universities are being taught by underpaid, non-benefit receiving part-timers. Yes, some schools do provide some benefits, and some adjuncts have unions to try to gain them better pay and benefits but to this point, that is not the case for most. According to the College Board's article "2006-07 College Costs: Keep Rising Prices in Perspective", the average tuition costs were as follows:

Four-year private	$22,218
Four-year public	$5,836
Two-year public	$2,272

Now let's assume that the average student takes 4 courses. So the four-year private student pays $5,554.50 per course; four-year public $1459 per course and two-year public $558 per course in tuition. For public schools which do get some public financial support, tuition is not the only revenue source so the cost per course is actually lower for the student but to keep the paying field even, we'll just figure tuition.

Now, consider that adjuncts seem to get paid around an average $3,400 a course with no benefits. So to equal pay for an adjunct at a two-year school it would take just about 6 students in the section to break even; a four-year public college or university would call for 2.3 students and a four-year private would need just a torso, not even a full student. Granted there are associated costs but this should provide a general notion that the number of 10 in a section for fiscal responsibility is just wrong. You can of course really figure the particular break even at your institution as follows:

RPC (revenue per student per course) =

$$\frac{\textbf{Tuition per student}}{\textbf{4}}$$

Number of students to break even =

$$\frac{\textbf{Cost of an instructor per section}}{\textbf{RPC}}$$

If a school can break even in the teaching of a course, it should always offer it. It should do so as a customer service to students and as a retention service to itself. A cancelled section loses students from their accurate perception of customer non-service. The student realizes he or she is not really important to the school. The college loses because students will drop out when courses are not available. Though universities may think they save money when they cancel an undersubscribed section, when one looks at the formulas above that belief is often proven untrue. The institution may very well either break even or make some money. Yes, we all know that colleges are not into it to make money but then why cancel sections students need to progress to graduation? Especially when there is no money lost?

Cancelling Retention

When course sections are cancelled, students begin to wonder if this college is a good choice and start the process that can culminate in dropping out. This is especially so when sections are cancelled for reasons of budget and cost reduction.

When a school cancels a section it usually does so late in the process. Very likely just the week before courses start or even in the first week of classes. Students have set up their lives around the schedule they created and in some cases, had approved by a faculty member or some official at the school. They set their work schedules around the course schedule. They set their transportation around the course schedule. Babysitting, if needed, is set to the course schedule. Their extra-collegiate obligations are planned according to the class schedule. Everything is set to revolve around the classes, days and times they selected in full faith that they will be provided. Then in the last week the school let's her know, too often by a notice on a board or the classroom where the course was to be; maybe a phone call, that the section is cancelled. "You must meet with your advisor immediately to choose another course." An academic version of bait and switch?

Maybe not, but it certainly is a wait and switch … to another school. First, the college has disrupted the student's plans and life. Really bad, no, the very worst customer service.

Then the next immediate question becomes, "Is this place worth it?" Students have paid their tuition and fees in full or have at least arranged to make sure their bills are paid. They may have received a discount called a scholarship but this is not seen as a price reduction; merely a part of the sales game like purchasing a car or TV at invoice. Sort of like, "If you buy today, I'm going to toss in this scholarship." Tuition sticker prices are simply starting points for negotiations. So whatever their final cost, they have paid in full so they expect to get full return. They expect the courses they need or desire will be available to them. In their minds, they bought the entire car and are not at all pleased when they hear that the tires will not be coming with it due to additional costs to the dealer. But when a school cuts sections that is like a car missing the tires.

The financial ROI or *worth it* question also goes to out-of-pocket cost since another term or semester will cost more actual tuition money. That pushes the student back down the taxonomy to the issue of "Can I afford it?" In turn, this basic concern can quickly take precedence in the student's mind thereby making cost a major retention factor once again. The student has to reconfigure affordability issues and until that lower level basic taxonomical concern is resolved, the student remains at risk for dropping out and transferring. Not necessarily to a less expensive school but one in which he or she feel the courses needed to graduate *on time* are available. That extra time is real money to the student in more than one way. First, the ability to afford more time in school. Second, the cost of lost earning. And, for some students costs to offset family requirements like babysitters.

Look back at the cost of a section formula. Before cutting a section, do the math. When you notice that the section will pay for itself, run it. If it could create a small loss, contrast the loss against an annual tuition received from a student because canceling the section will likely cause student attrition at some point. Is a small savings worth a large loss to the student and the school? The right decision will provide the school and student good customer service and help answer the question, "Can I graduate?"

Hierarchy Step 4: Can I Get a Job?

Now we come to one of the more divisive and hypocritical issues on a campus. It goes to the heart of the mission of an institution and why society supports higher education. It is an issue that many in higher education fault our students for holding. This is also one of the highest order concerns of all students and is a major deciding factor to attend or stay at a college or university. If students can answer it positively, they will attend and stay. If not, they will go elsewhere. Simply put, "Can I Get Job?"

Or to rephrase it as I have heard it from students "If I pay the money to go to this place, do the work, jump through the hoops required for me to graduate, will I get a job? A good job?"

The Job-Orientation of Students

The figures show that what motivated us to attend a college is still what motivates today's students to choose a school. And even more so. The annual study called *The American Freshman National Norms* by the Staff of the Cooperative Institutional Research Program (CIRP) at UCLA has been following the attitudes, motivators and beliefs of incoming freshmen for over 40 years. In the latest available CIRP report, 2006 freshmen indicated the following top reasons noted as very important in deciding to go to college:

	All	Men	Women
To learn more about things that interest me	76.8%	72.1%	80.6%
To be able to get a better job	70.4%	70.4%	70.4%
To get training for a specific career	69.2%	64.8%	72.7%
To be able to make more money	69.0%	71.9%	66.6%
To gain general ed and appreciation of ideas	64.3%	57.5%	69.9%
To prepare for graduate or professional school	57.7%	51.0%	63.1%

Three of the top five motivators to go to college focus specifically on a job resulting from going to college. The first motivator is also focused on jobs for students since they will major in areas of things that interest them and that major is most often the area in which they wish to work after college.

Again the 2006 CIRP shows the importance of a job from attending a school. The following CIRP chart adds strength to the argument listing the reasons for Attending *this* College by College Choice (percentages):

This college has a very good academic reputation

choices	*1st*	*2nd*	*3rd*	*4+ below*
	63.0*	49.9*	41.1*	30.5*

This college's graduates get good job

choices	*1st*	*2nd*	*3rd*	*4+ below*
	52.7*	44.9*	39.2*	31.3*

Source
http://www.epi.elps.vt.edu/Perspectives/06CIRPFSNorms.pdf)

Reputation is an extremely important aspect that leads to the initial choices. The second most important stated reason for choosing a school is that graduates get good jobs. There is indeed a relationship that students believe between getting into a name brand school (reputation) and getting a good job in a name brand company because one graduates from the institution. It is thus hard to separate out the first and second primary motivators since in the students' eyes, there are two parts of the same motivator – getting a good job.

Once the student is in a college and bills are or can be paid, when deciding to stay or leave, *this college's graduates get good jobs* rises right to the top after preceding basic concerns – affording and graduating – are answered. If a student is attending a school with a reputation for its graduates getting well paid jobs, students will often do all they can to stay there. They will stay at the university or college even if they are not able to respond with a positive answer to the final step in the hierarchy of decision-making, "Will I enjoy it?" There are cases in which a student even hates attending the school but believes graduating from it will lead to the good job or grad school, so he or she will most normally tough it out. A student I interviewed at a name brand school told me "I hate this place. I wish I had gone somewhere else but if I can just make it through another f---ing year, the name on the diploma will open doors. I can handle another year to get the job and money I want."

I got in. I can pay for it. I can see my way to graduation. Now, will it get me to where I want to go? Will I get a job, a good job after I graduate. If the answer is yes, students will be strongly motivated to stay as long as their corresponding motivation to get that job remains strong. We in higher education need to realize that. Students attend our colleges, our universities and our classes to do to what they must to graduate and get a job. We need to accept that reality at some level at least so we do not discourage students from staying at the institution or rejecting what we do. We should not denigrate students for doing what we did so we could get the position we sought in higher education.

College – AAA League for Jobs?

"Ahhh but, we in academia know that attending college just to get a job to make a lot of money is a crass, unintelligent motive for attending," says my colleague the humanities professor. To get a job! That's not what we are here for! Not why I went to school. The corporatization of colleges and universities is demeaning the role and value of education. If we were to agree to that as acceptable we would be lowering the value of higher education to become just a minor league for business, corporations and the economy.

We believe that higher education has been corrupted enough by the business-like attitudes of administrators and trustees. Trustees we can understand somewhat. They are from outside the academic community. In private colleges and universities they are usually business people, social and corporate big shots who can buy their way onto the boards. Why I am not exactly sure but they do. In not-for-profits, trustees are drawn from the same areas plus community and political activists who bring their or their sponsor's agendas onto the board. And the presidents have to cater to them and what they want done if they wish to keep the job.

We know that the models presidents and chancellors use and the way they make decisions are too often straight from the latest business best seller. The fad of the day. We've had them all from TQM to whatever is overshadowing a particular campus right now. This leads to hearing statements like the following from faculty: "They are trying to run the institution like it is a business and money and budgets are the most important thing around here. Much of that can be contributed to the outrageous salaries senior administrators pull down. No wonder they

think of themselves as CEO's and not college presidents. They are the ones who make this place feel so corporate as they suck up to corporations and businesses for donations. Administrators care more about bringing in money than the faculty or students. They seem to put their own interests before students and teaching.
And maybe a few science professors who spend their time looking for breakthroughs they can patent and make a fortune on. Oh yes, and athletics. Nothing but a big business with coaches making huge salaries and sponsorship deals. Maybe some TV and radio too. And well, the athletes are just interested in getting into the pros and making fortunes. But they do bring us school pride when they win. But the rest of us, NO!"

Well okay, maybe some biochemistry and genetic biology folks who do research paid for by big pharmaceuticals to find what they need so they can sell some pills and stuff. And yes, I suppose there may be some tech folks who write programs, widgets, invent stuff and processes and run their own companies when not in the classroom. The law and med professors do need to stay abreast of the real field so I suppose when they have their own practices and work as expert consultants, they are expanding their expertise and should be paid for it. There are some psychology, sociology and anthropology people who do that too. Some business professors may also. Not for the money or reputation of course. For intellectual growth. They use their real world consulting and businesses to strengthen their students' understanding of the real world of business.

Let's also realize they do not take time away from students either, since their classes are covered by TA's or adjuncts. Granted the TA's and adjuncts may not be as good as the experts but at least we are able to get them some work teaching courses for the name and faculty whose names and pictures are in the brochures attract students to the school. So the professors who may not teach all that much really do play an important role. By having their names listed in the university catalog, they help to bring students to the school where they will be taught by others. They are sort of the marketing bait to hook the students. They still get good education from the TA's and adjuncts that are switched in there. Granted, if the administration would just spend more money on more full-time faculty and salaries, this would not happen. But they have this business model that just hurts the institution.

Those who teach in other areas like engineering, business, criminal justice, technology and what we call the applied studies, do have another point of view. Here is where some of the CS Lewis divide comes in higher education. Sure, they teach theories and ideas, but they believe the students should be able to do something with the learning. That should not be what college is for. To focus on preparing students for careers and jobs is anti-intellectual. Simply because students are in college to get jobs and because society has supported education since it helps the economy, society and culture demeans the role of higher education to open students to new ideas and improve their ability to think, reflect, and enrich the culture and humankind. That's why students should come to college. Not for a job.

As an ex-English teacher, I know that I was not teaching people so they could get jobs when I assigned works such as Shakespeare, Faulkner, Dickinson, and Plato. My colleagues in many humanities areas such as philosophy, art, creative writing, theology and so on never taught to get students ready to get jobs after graduation. We were not concerned with business want ads such as philosopher wanted – *entry level position in growing firm needs philosopher; metaphysical background preferred.* That was not our job. Our job was to teach students all branches of philosophical endeavor and help them to get ready for graduate school. Maybe one of them would make it to the PhD and become a philosophy teacher. Which some might construe as a job I guess.

So if they did become a university professor, reading Plato was preparation for a job. But that would never be why I or my colleagues would have taught it. Not as job prep but as part of our own jobs…to work against job-oriented learning. That's a reason I went on to get a PhD after all. So I could work against the idea of college as career-prep. Except when I taught Technical Writing.

But to do what the technologists suggest is more training than learning. And training as we know is much more limited. Training is to make the respondent react in a certain way to a specific stimulus. This is stimulus A. When you see it, you are to do B. A therefore should yield B. That is training. But is training the realm of higher education?

Oh sure, maybe in community colleges and career schools but not universities. Community colleges and career colleges are there to train people to get a job. But in universities, there is a higher, non-career related mission. Training is for lower-level functions. For those who just want to get a job from their degrees. People like… well, doctors. Yes, they should be trained. That's good training. Stimulus A (blood flowing from a wound) should lead immediately to B (stop the bleeding). But then, people go to med school to become…..Well, to become a doctor which is a career, not a job.

Like I went to grad school and studied English to become a composition teacher in which I trained students to write which they did not want to do until they realized it applied directly to their future jobs. Once I could link it to their future work they had an interest. They finally became involved because writing could have an effect on their obtaining a good job. So they learned because…

Well, maybe there is some connection between college and work after all. In the students' minds at least.

We Were Our Students

Whether we want to admit it or not, accept it or not, we too went to college and university to get a job. Teaching is a job. We all went to college to become something. From early on in life we have been responding to the question, "What will you be when you grow up?" College is part of the answer. It helps us grow up as we go there to major in an area. That area is most always the one that we wish to work in as well even if it is to work in a university as a professor. Even art majors go to college to become better artists and maybe even sell their work. To make money and live. Just like our students. We really were no different. We chose schools based on whether or not they could get us into a good graduate school so we had a shot at a good first position that paid us money.

It never hurts to do something one enjoys for a job since we spend more time on the job than out of it quite often. That is why the CIRP found students saying they also came to school to study something that interests them as well as to get a good job. They want to do something they will enjoy while they study it so they can graduate and make money. Actually isn't that what we do every day we teach? Do something we enjoy and try to pass that pleasure on to our students? Isn't what we do trying to combine love of our subject and our work? And even if we teach or administer something that does not thrill us at this moment, don't we do that job so we can do other things we enjoy more? Just like many of our students know they may have to do something to get started in a career?

Of course there are some of us who will say that we only teach so we can have the time and money to do what we really want to do. And there are some teachers who try to become administrators to get out of teaching because they have a rather insane notion that administration is easier than teaching. And others will work very hard to get grants or release time to get out of teaching some sections. But that too is work that depended initially on getting a degree to be able to get a job in a college or university. Even if one teaches just to be able to study and read about what interests, teaching is still a job; a way to make an income and live, eat, and study or do something more pleasurable. By the way, students will say that they unfortunately know that some professors do not like teaching from the way such people teach.

They do not like teachers who are not engaged in their learning because they know that what skills and knowledge they might acquire are for their goals of graduating and getting a job. The only areas in which this may not be true are in required general education courses that are not seen to be somehow directly tied to their major. They will not concern themselves as much with these studies since they do not see the relationship to their career goals.

This reality has been noted by many, but it became recognizable as a universal when I was teaching English to French engineering students while a Fulbright fellow. They blatantly and vocally refused to do any homework at all or to prepare for any classes. Learning English did not apply to their studies and engineering goals. Lest anyone think this is just a French student's consideration, our students might not be as vocal about it but many English faculty can recall when their homework was not finished because students had some *important work* they had to do for their major classes.

When at the University of Massachusetts in Amherst, we attempted to make composition (or rhetoric as we called it) more relevant by relating all readings to major areas of study. So we had rhetoric for engineers, for pre-med, biology as well as technical writing courses, and so on. The scheme worked fairly well to get students to see some relationship between essays, writing and their lives. But even this approach was not fully embraced by students because it took away from time to focus on their real studies as I recall being told in numerous ways on evaluations for the courses. It did have some benefits, however, in that students, when they did get to the readings and writing did find some value in it.

It is important that colleges help keep students focused on college as a pathway to the job they want. More on how to do that later.

Hierarchy Step 5: Will I Like It?

When the four other hierarchical steps/decisions are satisfied in one or another way, the final enroll/stay question comes into play. This is a question that is less practical perhaps but becomes the primary concern for students once issues 1-4 are resolved. This decision question: Will I like it?

Colleges and universities almost always make the answer to this question a rather simplistic statement of a fairly complex issue. Most schools boil the enjoy issue down to one of two words – satisfaction and/or enjoyment. And they then implement these through activities the institution provides such as events or spectator sports. The belief is that if students *enjoy* things, they will be *satisfied.* But what one person likes or enjoys may not be what another does. What a school does in the belief that they will enjoy it often, nah, usually misses the mark by a wide margin.

Satisfaction?

Is the student satisfied? As it was put so well so many years ago by the Rolling Stones *I can't get no satisfaction* no matter what I try. Part of the reason is that no one knows what satisfaction really is. And when found, it is quite fleeting. What is satisfying to one is not necessarily satisfying to another. Could it be pleasure? But pleasure too seems so momentary and hedonistic. Like eating a good meal or even making love. When one is engaged in the act of eating and tasting good food or love is being made, it may be pleasurable but when it is done…it's over.

Satisfaction?

Fleeting at best. Not what one wants to base a customer service and retention program on. But so many will settle for it because it sounds right, and there are even surveys that claim to measure it. So maybe satisfaction is a good indicator of…of a snap shot of that moment in the students' time at the school. No more and maybe less.

But to give it its due, satisfaction is an important concept in most every discussion about customer service. We even have it in one of the 15 Principles of Good Academic Customer Service. It's number 12.

Satisfaction Is Not Enough and Never the Goal

Why not?

I'll give a personal example. I travel a great deal as I work with schools, colleges, universities and businesses that wish to improve their customer service and success. When I returned home after a ten day trip out, my wife who is a great cook made a fantastic meal. It was an Asian delight. Hot and sour soup. Green onion pancakes. Fried dumplings. Peking pancakes with meat topping and a vegetable stir fry. This was a meal that she had really worried and worked over; cutting the vegetables, filling the dumplings, sautéing the meat, rolling out the dough and just putting a great deal of time, preparation and emotion into it.

At the end of the meal, with the sink full of pots and pans that would need attention, she asked me, "How was it?" I smiled and replied that is was "quite satisfying".

I have been eating out a bit more than I used to now. Not sure why she was so upset? Most customer service books tell you that satisfaction is the goal…

Shouldn't satisfaction be more long lasting than a great meal anyhow? Well, maybe it really is happiness which we know even less about.

In his book *Satisfaction: The Science of Finding True Fulfillment (*Henry Holt and Company; 2005) Gregory Berns writes:

> Seeking satisfaction is distinct from chasing pleasure. Satisfaction is an emotion that captures the uniquely human need to impart meaning to one's activities. When you are satisfied, you have found meaning, which I think we all agree is more enduring than pleasure or even happiness (p. 244).

Many schools believe that intercollegiate athletics are a draw; something that will retain students since they enjoy watching sports. But the reports and studies do not support this in most schools. For the football and basketball powerhouses, there is some entertainment value certainly but when one drops below the top tier, the stands are often empty. Football is more for the alumni than for students unless the team is in Division 1 NCAA and is winning enough to be ranked.

Let Them Eat Football

Living in a city such as Columbus, it is clear to me that the Ohio State University football season is the center of life. When there is a home game, the city is fully animated. It would appear that students love going to a football game. Look at how the *Horseshoe* fills up completely every game…with mostly non-students.

Football tickets are for the non-student population. Football is not for the students. It is for the alumni, donors, significant supporters and administrators. In fact, when OSU was playing Florida for the national championship, only 1000 of the 16,000 OSU tickets were set aside for students. Only band members were assured a ticket. The team may have built school pride I suppose, but that eroded a bit after the loss. Moreover, there was no satisfaction at all with the team's performance and loss in the championship. And OSU's retention numbers were not affected except for the football players who elected to go into the draft early.

Football is not a true customer service for students or the campus community as recent testimony before the Knight Commission indicated.

Sports can indeed add to the school's image and help with recruitment. For instance, when I was Associate Provost at the University of Cincinnati, the basketball team made it into the Final Four. The University president, Joe Steger, said we could cut the marketing budget for the next year. The team's success would attract more applications.

And he was correct. But it did not have any effect on retention at the University.

When I was the Chancellor of a three-campus career college, I increased the number of intercollegiate sports teams from four to thirteen. Why? Because students wanted to play collegiate sports. It increased enrollment by over 140 students a year. Athletics helped our intake enrollment but did not help us with retaining population in general just as the Bearcats in the Final Four did not help UC retention. Activities like athletics do not add to retention unless the students are on the team, the band, a cheerleader or somehow involved with the team or activity.

The Engaging Feeling of Activity

There is that word *activity* again. And it is worth stating many times for that is the key to student's liking or not liking, enjoying or not enjoying their collegiate experience. It is the level of engagement a student feels that really counts, but not as defined by the National Survey of Student Engagement (NSSE), which looks at academic engagement alone.

Whether a student will like being at a school and likely stay has to do with how well the individual feels the institution actively engages him or her. Actively here means involving him or her in the institution in a way that makes the student feel valued and significant. Engagement that makes someone feel valuable can be as basic and as very powerful.

Just recall the Cheers TV show for a moment. People who came into the bar were made to feel as if they mattered; as if they had value. The simple act of welcoming Norm by calling out his name made him feel valued and important in the bar. Maybe nowhere else but there, he was NORM! The same is true for students. A school may not have everyone line up and shout out students' names as they enter a building of course for two reasons. First, most people would feel dumb and awkward doing that. And two, we generally do not learn the names, so we would get them wrong. The wrong name. Not a great welcome.

But it would be possible to at least recognize each student and employee/colleague. Not every character on Cheers received the Norm greeting but they all did get a "Hi" or "Hello", "Good to see yuh." and other such greetings. Every student can and should be given a "Hi (or Good morning). How are you today?" as we pass them in the halls or on the campus. And then we should actually listen for the response and even react to it. This simple activity creates engagement and leads to a person feeling a part of the university no matter what size it is. The more hellos from those identified with the college or university, the greater the active

imprinting on the student. The result is that students become happier to be at the college and that improves their sense of liking it. They feel a valued part and thus are greatly inclined to stay where they feel appreciated and respected.

Those Who Can Engage – Do

As I have studied all levels and types of schools, another key retention factor comes through. Students who are actually engaged in the school through activities such as work-study, part-time jobs, band, athletics, newspaper, frats and sororities, volunteering, and clubs tend to like the college more than those who don't. They are happier. These are all activities that provide the hello as well as an obligation and giving something. The responsibility is important since it ties the student to the activity and the activity to the school. It makes the activity important and in so doing makes the student more important. Even if the part-time job is sweeping a hall, that hall becomes *my* hall.

In fact, providing students part-time jobs to make tuition money is a better way to spend dollars than even scholarships. Scholarships may attract the student at first and help answer hierarchy concern 2 (Can I Afford It?), but the beneficial effect of a scholarship is short-lived. Once in, it is passé. If a school gave some scholarship in the form of part-time work, and even better, part-time work that could relate to the academic major, that investment is one in retention and happiness. Imagine a chemistry major helping in a lab or a sociology major assisting a sociology professor and so on. These activities would connect the students to the school much more than an initial handout.

In *Mistakes Were Made (but not by me)* (Hartcourt:2007), Tavris and Aronson discuss the *virtuous circles* that can create a spiral that starts with a deed that helps another or an organization and increases another's attachment to the person or organization.

> When people do a good deed…they will come to see the beneficiary of their generosity in a warmer light. Their cognition that they went out of their way to do a favor for this person is dissonant with any negative feelings they might have had about him. In effect, after doing the favor, they ask themselves: "Why would I do something nice for a jerk? Therefore, he's not as big a jerk as I thought he was – as a matter of fact, he is a pretty nice guy who deserves a break." (p.28)

Students who work at or participate in the university will also feel the institution is a positive place to be.

The truth of this can be seen and heard in what Jeffrey Docking, President of Adrian College in Michigan did to increase enrollment at the school. He added activities such as band, athletics and other co-curricular activities that would attract and retain students. President Docking also did give every activity an enrollment goal which made it important for the coaches, for instance, to create a Cheers atmosphere in the Division III, no scholarships college. Without scholarships, the coaches had to use personal attachment and customer service to attract students so they could meet their goals. The result, a 91% increase in freshman enrollment that also translated into retention.

While some feared academic standards would suffer, the effect has been the opposite. The freshman class has a higher academic profile, and the percentage of freshmen who returned to second semester jumped from 77 to 93 – the highest retention rate in the school's history.

Adrian is providing students the opportunity to engage in something they enjoy and the college at the same time. They get something out of playing sports, being in the band, writing for the newspaper and so on. They invest in these activities. These activities also engage them in service to the activity and the school thus increasing their ties to the college.

So, there is one customer service that colleges can provide the students that will also increase retention and happiness. That is the service of being active in the school and being able to serve it.

Why Students Leave a College

AcademicMAPS has surveyed and interviewed 640 students a year for the past six years after they had dropped out of a school to find out why they left. The passage of a year as well as our non-affiliation with any particular college or university provided the students the distance

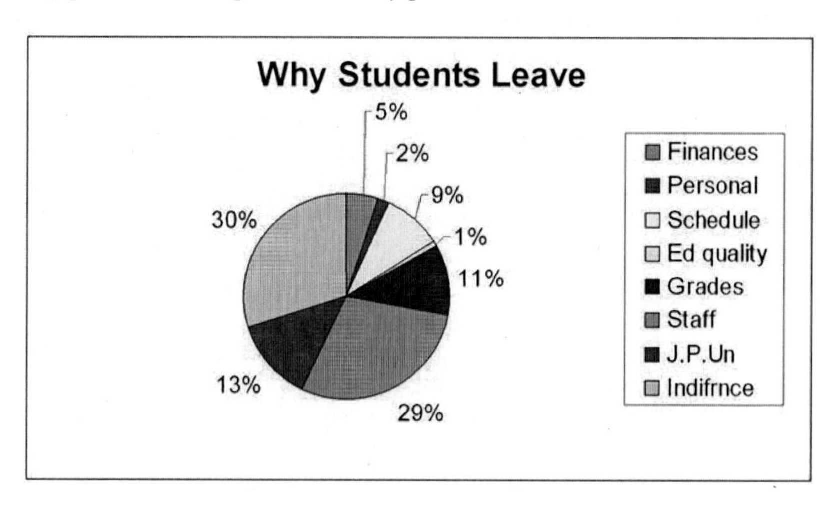

and anonymity for more open discussion on actual attrition causes. The students were randomly selected. They were often at their new college, one where we had been hired to audit or present training. The above chart is a compilation of that research on why students *really* leave a school.

What we discovered is not what ex-students might tell a school official since they will generally play to the interviewer during their meetings with your exit counselor (if the school has one). Students will most often intone *personal reasons* as their justification for leaving the school. They assume the interviewer will either not dig into their personal lives or will buy the vague soap opera they spin, because they know we are basically voyeurs rather than intervention people. We do love a good story, even if it may not be true or the real reason the student is leaving. But then again, if it is a *personal reason,* most officials are happy to accept that for two main reasons. First, most colleges accept that personal reasons are a valid basis to leave school. Second, if students leave for personal reasons, neither the college nor the individual are really accountable for some failure in the department, school or our so-called systems. The institution cannot be held responsible if they leave for personal reasons, can we?

But when AcademicMAPS personnel dug a bit, it was discovered that the personal problems fell into a few major categories which indicate that departing students do have a sort of personal issue – a customer service issue – with the school. Most often, they said they didn't like the way they were treated and that they took that personally. They tell us that they felt the school was indifferent toward them as a person, as a learner, or as anything but tuition revenue. A very common statement was, "All they seemed to care about was me paying on time." This feeling of apathy from the school is the major reason 30% of the students said they were motivated to leave. This feeling violates our *Customer Service Principle 1* "Everyone wants to attend Cheers University where everyone knows your name, and they're awfully glad you came." Once they feel you do not care, they are on the way out the door over to Gary's Old Towne Tavern.

The second major reason students quit a school is dissatisfaction with how the staff treats them. Staff here means anyone who works at the college from maintenance people on down. Administrators are staff. Faculty are staff. Everyone is in a staff relationship to the clients, the students. Everyone is there, or should be there, to serve and meet the needs of the students, the school's primary customer.

Generally students will point out some clerical, management or administrative staff as the primary poor customer service villain. This is because students are more lenient with faculty in general until one of them blows it big time. Sort of like the belief voters have that their local representative is honest and sincere until caught in an airport men's room. Then all hell breaks loose. The college's landing strip becomes filled with helicopter parents and it's "threaten to call the lawyers time." Students want to believe their teachers care about them even if they don't seem to really show it much. They will remember the slights from the clerical staff and try to overlook indifferent even cruel Paper Chase Charles W. Kingfield type faculty members until they realize that these faculty are hurtful and not just demanding. But that can and will change if the professor shows his or her cruelty in the grade a student gets after putting in what he or she felt was hard work and effort. Grades have become the coin of the realm for students, and they believe they are paying for them in one or another way – study and tuition. How many times have you heard students refer to how much they are paying and how much they deserve since they pay so much to go there? Moreover since a major motivator for staying in a school is getting a job, lower than expected grades are a disincentive to many students. Students who do not receive what they believe was their effort in their grades often feel they have been or are being maltreated, and they will not stay and pay for that. So they leave.

A quick note here. The belief that customer service is equated to giving easy grades is not true. Customer service is not in the grade itself but in a combination of the effort for the grade and the assistance provided to be able to achieve a higher grade. The situation is anometic .Students who do not put in the effort or seek help accept what grades they get. Students who make a sincere effort expect that the college will provide the services to help them succeed with an acceptable grade. The services such as tutoring by qualified tutors who can actually help students learn the material, review assistance, additional study material and supplementary opportunities to understand the information or achieve the skill needed to obtain an acceptable grade are customer service.

When students leave a college for what they categorize as personal or financial reasons, it does not mean they don't go to another school, although they may tell you they have a problem that calls for taking time off. They don't want to insult the interviewer with negative reports about his or her colleagues or the school. The students avoid this not because they are afraid of hurting someone's feelings, but because they don't want to hear a defense or excuses. They want to get in and out of what they feel to be an unsettling experience as quickly and painlessly as is possible. They also will claim personal reasons since they do not wish to explain their real reasons for leaving if they can avoid it.

Confrontation is not a sought after event. People will do all they can to avoid it at all costs.

The 2006 NSSE study indicated that over 60% of students attend more than one college prior to graduation. No indication of how many people try more than one school and quit higher education completely. That should not comfort people if their school is one that loses more than receives students. Misery likes company, but there are no revenue dollars in the misery of losing a large portion of enrollment, especially to those who get laid off to meet budget as a result of too many students transferring out to another school

The third major reason students attrit is they are just plain unhappy with the school. The institution has spent so much time and money to get them to come that the school forgets it is much easier and much less costly to keep a student than to recruit and enroll them to begin with. Before classes, there are numerous communications, well planned activities at orientations, events, even celebrations to make sure the students will show up. Once classes start, most schools seem to forget to keep up the effort that says we are glad you came.

Even if a school tries to maintain a focus on making students feel welcome during freshman year, it almost always ends at most every school as soon as sophomore year rolls around. Now, it is assumed, the students are mature, focused and will remain satisfied with the college. That false assumption leads to more dropouts. Just look at the chart and it will be seen that the third primary reason for dropping out is the students were just plain unhappy. Taking away the focus after freshman year is a sure way to add to potential dissatisfaction. Once any institution provides good customer service, it cannot, it should not be taken away. And it is so simple to maintain, actually. In fact, all the reasons for leaving a school can be alleviated rather easily. How? Through improving customer/client service and providing staff some training in the same.

In summary, when one thinks about the chart above, it indicates that 72% of students leave a college – your college – for customer service reasons. Thirty percent leave due to what they perceive as indifference. Twenty-nine percent decide to drop out from staff problems, primarily confrontation and lack or response and 13% leave simply because they are just plain unhappy at the college.

These are essentially customer dissatisfaction issues. If your institution could increase satisfaction, i.e. customer service, it would reduce attrition. That would correspondingly become a significantly positive factor for the revenue and bottom line. "How much money to the bottom line?" would be the next question followed by, "How does one figure the financial effects of attrition and retention?"

CSFs: Customer Service Factors

There are three primary Customer Service Factors (CSFactors™) AcademicMAPS has formulated to help universities, colleges and career schools figure out the loss or gain from retention and attrition. The CSFactors are provided as formulas schools can use to figure out how much revenue they are losing or could and would gain if they focused on improving service to students. The formulas are quick methods to understand the financial power of retention coming out of customer service to students. Placing your college or university's actual numbers into the formulas will quickly bring forward the real power of retention to positively affect the revenue and future of the institution.

They could also be applied to employee retention, another significant revenue and service issue, but here we focus on students. The formulas were developed and tested from the research AcademicMAPS conducted during college service audits, workshops, presentations, retreats and other services provided to higher education as well as just pure research.

CSFactor 1: The Cost of Attrition

CSF1 helps a college figure out how much revenue/money it is losing from its actual attrition. CSFactor 1 is stated as:

CSF1 = [(P X A= SL) X T]

In the formula, **P** represents the total school population; not just the starting fall freshman number. Most schools use the fall incoming freshmen number and that is an error. The assumption is that attrition occurs most in the first six weeks of the freshman year. That may have some validity for the freshman year but the reality is that students are leaving colleges and universities in any one of the average six-plus years of a four-year degree and in the four-plus average years of a two-year degree. Students leave a school throughout their experience at the college. In fact, some schools are beginning to realize this and worry about the sophomore bubble.[1] But they really need to worry about the *super soph sluff, the rising junior jilt, the junior jump, super junior split, the fourth year flee* and so on. Every year, every semester, in fact every day is a chance for a student to drop out. Colleges need to be concerned with every student every day of their attendance, for it could be his or her last. So we look at the total population.

Annualized tuition is the number a school should use to figure its real attrition. Not the retention between the first and second semester or the freshman and sophomore years which are very popular ones. That leaves out all the students who already dropped out before the end of the second term or semester. That number fudges failure. For instance, if a college began a year with 100 new freshman and 99 left in week one but the remaining student stayed the whole year and returned for a sophomore year, the freshman to sophomore percentage would be 100%.

In CSF1, **A** equals attrition. Again not just from freshman but an annualized attrition rate. And this rate is to include ALL students who leave for any reason. It does not matter if the student says he or she will be back. They are not in the population bringing in revenue until they actually do return. If they pay a place holding fee, that does not count them as a student until they are actually back in classes.

Fudge with the numbers if you have a need for delusion or are insecure, unethical or want to keep the Board feeling better, but when you use the formulas, be fully honest. It will help you understand why the budget is not working or may suddenly implode. No one likes surprises, especially ones that have parentheses around them in the budget and lead to freezes, cuts and the like. Using the formulas honestly can help forecast a reality to avoid surprises and initiate work on retaining students to maintain fiscal and operating health.

SL stands for students lost annually from total population and revenue production. And **T** equals annual tuition at the school.

So here is what showed up when we analyzed CSF1 for Mammon University. You may know it. Its motto is *Omnes Por Pecunia. Anything for a Buck.*

Its total population was 500 students

Annualized attrition was at 39.6%

So **SL** (students lost annually) was 198.

Times an annual tuition of $13,000.

So, the formula becomes:

[(500 x 39.6% = 198) x $13,000] = a revenue loss of ($2,574,000)

To carry this forward, we can plug in other numbers and see how an increase in retention could add to the bottom line and thus the ability to pay for full time faculty, staff, their benefits, increases for adjuncts, instructional equipment, tutors, research release, new curricula and programs, maintenance, and so on. All those pesky costs that make a college or university better.

If attrition dropped by 5% for this school, and we substitute 5% increased retention for attrition percentage in the formula.

CSF1 = [(500 x 5% = 25) x 13,000] = $325,000 more revenue

Plug your school's numbers in, and see how increasing retention affects your budget and instructional strength while attrition will sap the ability to meet budget and mission.

CSF2: Figuring Real Admissions and Attrition Costs

There is a universal law, or if there isn't there should be one that it would take less energy to sit on a flagpole than to climb it. Seems logical. Climbing it numerous times to gain different views would require burning more calories than shinnying up once and sitting there to look around for the views. Yet there are certainly those who seem to have not learned that lesson. Colleges that have not yet focused on the value of retention – which can be increased through some simple customer service training – too often rely on the ill – conceived churn and burn approach.

Keep bringing in ever increasing numbers of new students and don't worry if they just drop out never to return. Just get some more.

These schools make admission folks in particular climb the pole over and over, burn calories, the late night compact fluorescents, and just plain burn out trying to meet ever-increasing admission goals. You'd think some universities had never heard of flag pole sitting on a pillow called retention. Or the stabilizing element of customer service that creates the cushioning in the pillow. Or ever concerned themselves with little issues like revenue, budgets and paying for things. Or the energy-saving and budget building value and cost-savings of retention. Flagpole climbing not only burns off calories and people, but piles of revenue through admission and student acquisition costs.

CSF2: FGE's and Admission Costs

Another simple reality here. Every student a college enrolls costs it money to do so. And it can be a significant amount of money too! Every student retained costs from nothing to quite little. At the 2007 Snowmass Institute, a participant stated that her university had calculated the cost of retaining a student at $35 each. That is an extremely minor cost especially when placed alongside of the revenue lost from just one student leaving.

A study we complete two years ago found that the average cost of enrolling a student is $5,460. This study of 40 randomly chosen colleges, universities and career schools included ALL cost of enrolling a student. Most colleges just look at direct marketing costs per student and forget about all the associated costs. They divide marketing and advertising, maybe lead costs too, by the number of students and *voila* – a miscalculation.

The real costs of enrolling a student include the direct marketing expenditures like brochures, ads, printing, but also the marketing staff, advertising, publications, admission staff, clerical people, travel, orientation, printing, allocated time and effort from bursar, registrar, academics, counseling, advising, student services, financial aid, orientation, registration, admission committee time and costs, and so on. And we cannot forget to include mailings, postage, emails, phone calls, website and so on and on and on. Fixed capital costs associated with most all of this add another 7-9% on the average. The AcademicMAPS study did not figure in average scholarship granted which is also a cost factor. There are in fact very few parts of a college that are not involved at some point and time in admitting, enrolling and starting.

AcademicMAPS also found that 39 of the 40 schools were not including all students who had made inquiries to the college in calculating their acquisition costs. Every time a student is responded to there are costs. These all add to the time and considerable expenditures. For some schools, the cost of recruiting a student actually outweighs the tuition received from them in the first semester and for some even into the first semester of the second year. Those in the publicly assisted category offset some and three publicly assisted schools offset all the loss from some public financial assistance based on an unduplicated headcount formula. But even with public assistance all schools still lose money on student acquisition when the student drops out. This is especially so if the student leaves in the first semester or term before providing tuition and fees at least equal to the acquisition costs. And every student who leaves must be replaced with at least another at another additional expenditure of $5,460. But it usually requires more than one replacement student and associated acquisition costs.

Schools normally look at their enrollment and population in terms of FTE, full-time equivalent students. For attrition and retention purposes it is necessary to consider the FGE (full-time graduate equivalent). An FGE is equal to how many students it takes for the school to get one student through the entire degree program and graduate. In fact, at an average annualized attrition of 32%, it will take at least 3-4 students acquired to get one FGE at a two-year school. Six to eight will be needed at a four-year school, with an average graduation period of four to five years. If average graduation is more than five years, it may be required to add another admission to get the four year FGE.

The FGE is actually a more important number than the FTE in a number of growing ways. More and more, politics and society are calling on colleges and universities to prove they are effective. And the growing success determinant is graduation numbers – not starts or current population. This is because society sees college as a place in which the leaders and workers for tomorrow are prepared. The number of people who graduate and then can enter the workforce or become service providers of one or another type is also the surest indicator statistic of how well a school is meeting its own mission. Just look at your own mission and note how you too focus in one or another way on graduation and success.

Population may be what we set out budgets on, but success is what we are judged upon. It is sort of like if the college or university has a football or basketball team. Being able to gather enough players together can get you into the game, but the college and alumni judge the team and the school's investment on the success of the team. Not how many games they play, but how many they won. And that is becoming the analogy for population and support as well. Not just how many a school brings in but how many it graduates. And for figuring ROI this is a significant concept as well.

CSF 2: Using The Formula

CSF2 = [SL x CA = -E) + CSL1]

In CSF 2, **SL** represents the number of students lost. **CA** is the cost of acquiring a new student. so **- E** represents the enrollment dollars lost. Therefore, **CSF2** calculates the total revenue lost.

So using the numbers from the prior Mammon University example:

(198 x $5,460) = ($1,081,080 + $2,574,000) = -$3,655,080

This school has lost almost 200 students along with $3,655,080. If it had retained the 198 students, it would have saved the $3.6 million. Even if it did spend $35 a student to retain the dropouts, that would have cost them $6,930. If we extend that cost out four years, it is found that $27,720 is still just a bit less than $3.6 million.

Seems again that retention saves while attrition costs – and costs one hell of a lot of money.

But let's not ignore the human costs of people working very hard to bring students into the school just to see them leave. We have not even worked in the costs of replacing admission and enrollment people who simply burn out from the ever-increasing new student recruitment goals. The loss of trained and successful people should not be discounted at all.

Every time an employee leaves there are not only dollars consumed in replacing that person but also days and weeks of not having the productivity from the individual. The time it takes a college or university to advertise, recruit, select and train the new employee – as well as the ramping out period before he or she can be successful in the position – is considerable. Weeks and months can go by with productivity loss taking away from the school's ability to meet its goals. Even if the remaining people step up their efforts and hours, there are deficits generated not to mention increasing the remaining employee's burnout potential. And since most managers in higher education really are quite weak or worse when it comes to recognizing and rewarding employees, those who have to make up the lost productivity become the next to consider finding another job. We never should ignore the psychological pain of climbing the ever-growing flagpole every start when they should be able to just sit there every so often and enjoy the retention view.

CFS3: A Cost or A Bonus

A school loses an average of 12% of its potential enrollments as soon as a prospective student makes actual contact with it. Whether that connection is made through the website (which was created by the Sites That Hoover Group for most colleges), by telephone, email, or make it onto campus, 12% of probable enrollments are lost with tangible contact. And these potential students are most often seriously considering enrolling in the college. They may have even been making that contact to do so. They had found enough interest in the school to explore it and considered applying or enrolling. Then they made contact.

They may have tried to navigate a web site created not for the user but the college community. They could not find basic information efficiently. The information they finally located did not address their needs or questions. They tried to email for information, but the directory listed the last seven campus telephone numbers and no email addresses or direct active links. When they arrived on a page, the link was broken so they were stranded. The language was some sort of secret code known primarily to those immersed in academic-ese. The college catalog was there but since it did not have a user friendly program like Leadwise™ it could not be searched or supply them what information they wanted.

They may have phoned the school and were greeted by a phone tree that told them the options had changed so listen closely as if this would be an admission's quiz. Then the annoying electronic voice made sure the prospective student could not find the office she needed or had so many numbers to remember that he failed the memory test. Or an indifferent receptionist began the greeting by asking them to wait and listen to music elevators rejected or a canned advertisement for the school. Then the receptionist connected the caller to an office in which people let the calls go to voice mail and erased the calls at the end of the day.

The potential students came to the campus and drove around trying to figure out where the office they wanted to get to was located. The signs, if there were any, only listed places by the building name which is no help to a prospective student. Then if the prospect finds the building with the office she is seeking, it took a long frustrating time to find a parking space because the signs all let her know, "This lot reserved for..." When she did find a spot in Lot C, there were no maps to direct her back to the building she had so much trouble finding.

If he made it to the building, there was a lack of internal signage, so he then wandered the halls hoping someone would be willing to help him. But the college employees are too busy or distracted to stop and help a clearly confused student who should know his way around anyhow. After going into a couple of offices where the secretary tried to be helpful but was not sure where the person or office he was seeking is, he was sent to yet another wrong location. By the time he did find the correct office after the traditional campus shuffle, he missed his appointment and had to make a new one for another time. And, well, there are other colleges after all.

In these ways and others, actual contact convinces 12% of probable students that they would no longer be interested. That leads to

Customer Service Factor 3

CSF3 = [(AE x12%=EL) x tuition]

IE represents the Initial actual Enrollment
12% is what is lost on initial contact
EL is the Enrollment Lost and
T once again is the tuition.

So, continuing with Mammon U. (which has just written a formal complaint to US News and World Report for not including it in the top tier of colleges and universities which everyone at Mammon knows is an error and just makes education a commodity in the minds of the public which should care about purer motives while Mammon knows that a top ranking will improve its application flow and lead to meeting enrollment objectives while reducing advertising expenditures and so it can consider raising tuition for more revenue because it can still attract a class at the higher cost from the increased ranking…)

Mammon's original enrollment is budgeted at 200 in the Fall. They aren't there just yet so the admissions folks are beating the bushes and going through every potential applicant they have. They are at 180 enrollments at this point so the CFO is concerned that the budget they created back in June – and assured the Board they would meet – will not be met for the third year in a row. And the president is now reading the <u>Chronicle of Higher Education</u> starting with the career section. If Mammon does not find the last 20 enrollments, CSF3 will be calculated like this:

CSF3 [(200 x 12%% = 24) x $13,000] = ($312,000)

The point that may make immediate impact if you are not an admissions or enrollment management person is the revenue loss of $312,000. That is a solid amount of lost revenue which may lead to starting the year with some budget, employee, equipment, maintenance or other cuts. That will usually catch most everyone's attention. Everyone hates cuts.

But a person in admissions would be thinking, "*Merde,* if we didn't lose some of the potential applicants, we would not have just hit the 200 goal, we would have exceeded it by 4! We would be celebrating instead of commiserating and getting the job network invigorated again." The formula could have shown

[(200 +12%% = +224) x $13,000] = + $312,000

Consider again that the 12% loss of students is from potential enrollments that contacted the school to take the next step to apply and enroll. These are students the school had already attracted sufficiently that they were ready to make a commitment. But they were finally lost due to poor customer service. They should never have been dissuaded. Customer service would have saved them.

Checking Your School's Health

The CSFactors™ can be used to determine how much attrition is costing a school. Conversely, they can also show how much revenue could be realized if a college focuses on keeping students enrolled. The negative numbers yielded by the formulas could all be indicators of how much money would be gained by focusing on one consistent area – customer service.

Not the surface issues that one might read about in any of the commercial books that discuss one or another method that will help a store sell more widgets or market more business services. A customer service that is appropriate to the unique enclaves we know as colleges, universities and career colleges. A customer service that recognizes that our clients/customers are not at the school for a unitary single purchase event such as buying a pair of shoes, but to learn and grow so they can obtain the career and future they see for themselves. It is a customer service that is not expressed in a set phrase such as "Hi, I'm Dr. Brown. I will be your professor today. Can I start you off with an intellectual appetizer?"

It is a customer service more akin to the relationship of a doctor and patient. The patient realizes that he or she needs assistance to get healthier and stronger. The patient thus recognizes weaknesses that will need attention and even correction. He must also be willing to follow the directions and course of action the doctor prescribes. The patient is also to take the prescribed actions at the time the doctor says to and complete any and all additional therapy conscientiously. The patient is also expected to make all appointments and be prepared to review the time between meetings when requested, so the doctor can understand progress or lack of it. This is so the patient can pass all the medical tests and receive a good report.

On the other hand, the patient places very important items in the keeping of the doctor – body, soul and a healthy future. The doctor is required to let the patient know what is needed even if the remedy calls for discipline, hard effort and following instructions until the full course of treatment is completed. The doctor must be honest and conscientious in all she does, but that does not exclude the patient's demand that she do so using a personal, polite and respectful approach (no matter how popular House, MD is on TV). The doctor is also called upon to provide the most up-to-date remedies available; old, yellowed, out-dated prescriptions and approaches won't do. And the doctor is expected to be available for extra care, consultation and appointments if the patient has questions, is having trouble or simply needs assurance or additional discussion of the remedy.

And the patient does expect that his or her needs will be met and that includes a friendly acknowledgement from the receptionist, nurses and the doctor herself. Patients all want to believe they are important enough for the doctor to smile at and remember their name and medical chart without having to read through the chart each time. And he does not want to have to wait too long to be able to see the doctor. He believes his time is as important as the doctor's and just because insurance is covering some of the cost does not mean he is any less important. After all, the doctor is making what appears to be a good living from the money received from the patient.

Finally, the patient really believes he is coming to the doctor to get better and stronger so he can achieve his goals in life. If at any time the patient believes that the doctor is not focused enough on his goals, does not really care about him or does not see that he is getting better, he will look for a second opinion and a new doctor.

A doctor builds a solid practice with a long list of loyal patients that provides her a very good income if she fulfills all the customer service expectations above. And most importantly, if she makes patients better so they live the healthy productive lives they seek.

A college, university or career college will retain students providing it receives the revenue and loyalty it needs to be able to perform and meet its mission through a similar customer service focus. And the most important customer service is meeting student expectations that they will be prepared to graduate, get a good job and meet the goals they have set. If a school does that, the CSFactors™ will all become positive numbers.

Return on Investment (ROI)

Learn and Earn; Not Churn and Burn

What are the four basic indicators of a successful school in its operations and well-being?

Indicator 1: Population.

Indicator 2: Population.

Indicator 3: Well, no surprise here – Population.

Indicator 4: Customer service levels.

If a school is able to maintain and grow its population, then all is in order. Note I said population. Not admissions. Hitting admission numbers does not indicate the health of the institution, particularly if a school is losing 30 percent or more of its students. Simply put, if a sales team sells 100 pet rocks on Monday, but by next week 30 are returned, then how many were really sold? The sales team may be celebrating hitting *its* goal but the CFO is dying because the lost revenue and costs associated with selling and processing returns have basically wiped out any profit. All the company has learned is that the pet rock can be sold but has very little customer retention power and may just have been sold in a way that can lead to bigger issues down the line.

Customer service and a student's belief that his investment in this school will be met if not exceeded in three types of ROI are the key to population. If students and staff do not believe their *F-ROI* (financial return on investment); *E-ROI* (emotional return on investment); and *A-ROI* (associative return on investment) are being positively impacted by the customer service level they receive, population is in trouble. And the school's well-being, finances and morale are also in trouble.

Population stability and growth are primary indicators. Hitting retention says the students are pleased with the school, their education, and the experience. Faculty members are happier because students are more receptive to instruction, do their work on time, and are more compliant with faculty directions, according to studies discussed in the January 2006 newsletter *Great Service Matters* (www.greatservicematters.com). Students are even pleased to go to class. Faculty morale also increases since it is much easier to teach happy and committed students. The business officer is pleased because the college will maintain solid positive revenue, on-time collections and an operating margin/EBITDA (earnings before interest, taxes, depreciation, and amortization). And believe it or not, our research indicates that if students are pleased with the customer service they receive, a school can even raise tuition and not suffer adverse effects in student acceptance.

How to do all this?

Focus on customer service.

As long as students, faculty and administration are all pleased with the school, admission targets might be missed, and that is not unusual in the tight competitive market all schools are trying to draw students from, yet revenues, margins, and financial goals can be met with population maintenance/retention through increased customer service. Furthermore, if everyone is happy and population retention leads the way, admissions may have a more achievable goal. That can lead to reduced stress and will lead to fewer angry admissions people. Angry admissions staffers can hurt admissions, retention, and the whole school as the public questions the school.

I had the bi-polar pleasure of working with a school that had missed almost all of its admission goals for four years but succeeded in most of its financial goals. It worked hard to meet recruitment goals and felt crushed when it fell short. Yet, when I was able to get the focus on retention and population during the three years I led the school, we hit most all of our margin and revenue goals. How? The school worked hard to maintain the population it had through a strong and sincere focus on customer service to students and faculty, as well as focusing on meeting the three ROI's the students expected.

The Three ROI's

Return on Investment is normatively a financial formula. ROI = Return/Investment yielding a hoped-for positive percentage. The basic ROI formula works with colleges and customer service not as a financial plus or minus percentage basis, but on more personal and psychological formulations composed of feelings and perceptions that the investment is worthwhile. If it is, the student is comfortable, even happy, and stays. If the student does not feel there is at least a financial, emotional, and associative equity between what he or she invests and what the school returns to him or her, there will be a negative sense of ROI and the student will likely leave or trudge through unhappily, bad-mouthing the school whenever the chance arises.

F-ROI (financial return on investment) works on two levels for students. The first F-ROI is the perception of whether or not, "I am getting my money's worth. Do I feel that the money I am paying to the school is being well spent on me?" The second F-ROI is whether or not the student believes that staying at the school will finally lead to the job and career that he or she came to the school to acquire.

There then are two separate but related equations at work. For F-ROI the evaluation is a judgment of the value of a wide grouping of what might at first seem to be disparate issues that range from the obvious (such as perceived value of classroom instruction, whether or not faculty seem to care if students understand and are learning, to how staff treat students and even important physical issues such as facilities, parking, lighting, and so on). One college I studied had a low collective student sense of the F-ROI (41 percent positive) with the two major concerns being *weak instructors* and *dirty bathrooms*. The F-ROI was raised a quick sixteen points by cleaning and painting the bathrooms. And retention also went up by 4.3 percent that semester.

The F-ROI that goes to future career returns on the investment is not simply a concern of financial investment through tuition, fees, books, etc., but the feeling that "this school will help me obtain the job I am going here to get." Students must believe that the college will not only assist them in their job search but the school's position and reputation will facilitate obtaining that first job. If the school helps the students prepare for applying for jobs or, even better, if the school has an active outreach to students on careers and assistance in locating possible jobs, the F-ROI will stay in the positives.

E-ROI (emotional return on investment) refers to the emotional investment that a student and that student's family make in the school. When a student decides to attend a college, that person is making a commitment based on an expected return on investment such as the financial ones spoken of above. But he or she is also making an emotional decision as well that is somewhat akin to an engagement. Trust, attachment, and an allegiance between the student and the school are developed in the student's mind and feelings. The student is making a pledge to the school that he or she expects will be returned. That pledge is, "I will trust you to do right by me. I will put my education and thus my future in your hands. I will trust you to treat me fairly and provide me an honest opportunity to learn and get that job I want to love." Very few, if any, students will simply make a cold business-like decision to apply, taking a chance of rejection and then finally accept the offer of engagement from a college without emotion involved. Social psychology experiments have indicated that even if applicants were not sure about the school at some time, upon acceptance, they will begin to look more favorably on the school and decide that it was a better school and choice after all.

Though students are transferring from colleges at a record rate and attending more than one institution to graduate, according to studies such as the 2006 National Survey of Student Engagement, students enter a school with a belief that they will complete a degree at that school. Students who attend a two-year school, for instance, enter with the intention of transferring to another school *after* graduation, yet many do not stay to graduation. They leave.

Why? Because they fall out of love with the college. They do not perceive that their emotional investment is being returned by the school. The students I have interviewed have indicated two major perceptions of why they fall out of love with a school. First, they say, "The school only cares about me for the money they get." They see the school as putting money ahead of the students (too many adjunct faculty, not enough sections of courses, poor scheduling, canceling classes at the last minute, not enough staff, aggressive bursar and collections letters and more). Second, the school does not reach out to them and show it cares about the student as a person with integrity and needs (can't find faculty during office hours, can't get extra help when needed, faculty do not seem to realize students have lives too, administrators don't care or solve problems, staff are cold or rude, no one smiles, students get the run-around also known as the shuffle, issues go unresolved or with just a decision that is unexplained, etc.).

A-ROI (Associative Return on Investment) can be understood through the sense that by going to this school, "I am saying something about me and my values and character. By attending I am increasing my social standing. I am investing my standing and self-value in the school." This can be seen in the clothes that students wear, especially collegiate or sports-related hats, tees, and sweatshirts. When a student wears a T-shirt, for example, with the name of a college adorning the front, it is done to make a statement to the world about the wearer. If a student is wearing the name of a college such as Harvard , University of Michigan, or the University of Miami, or one of the other name-brand colleges, he or she is trying to tell the viewer to associate him or her with the school – even if they do not go there. It is a statement that the student wants to be associated with the strength and value of the school's name.

The student is saying, "I am part of this school and it makes me feel good." It improves value and recognition. That is why when I was associate provost at the University of Cincinnati (Ohio) and the Bearcats men's basketball team made it into the NCAA Final Four, applications shot up. People wanted to be associated with a successful basketball team/school. One way a school can judge if its associative value is up or down is by counting the amount of logo- or name-laden clothing that is sold in the bookstore. If students want others to know they go to the school, they will wear the association.

The ROI on association can be a strong one if the student feels that the school is well known and respected in the community. If it is not, the school can create strong associative value by providing excellent service to the student, who will then take pride in the institution, even if others do not know it is so good. A school can overcome lack of current recognition if the services are strong enough. "It is an excellent school and I know it, so I feel great being associated with it even if you haven't heard of it." This is then a more personal ROI but still a very important one. Lose the student's belief in the school and the A-ROI drops. When that happens, the student does not want to be associated with the school and is a certain candidate to transfer.

The customer service consulting I have been doing since 1999 makes me realize that there are 15 simple customer service principles to changing a school from a *churn and burn* attitude (characterized by the thinking that all we have to do is keep enrolling them, bring 'em in the front door and if they just walk through and out the back door, we just go after even more students to make up the difference) to a *learn and earn* approach.

Learn and Earn

Learn and Earn is a client/customer service focus that is a variation on successful models of many thriving businesses created by AcademicMAPS for higher education. The basics of the model focus on what should be a self-evident idea – when you attain a customer, do all you can to retain him so you do not have to replace him. Furthermore, the objective is to lower the required number of new customers to balance the budget while increasing loyalty and investment in the school. The goal is to up-sell students (i.e., two-year degree students stay to go for a four-year degree; bachelor students continue on for a graduate degree; graduates come back for additional courses such as license prep and professional/personal growth courses and greater alumni involvement and support are evident).

Not retaining and not up-selling students are costly for a college. Every new recruitment brings significant start-up costs that must be recouped and/or amortized over the whole business. A college has to bring in an average of six new students for every student lost before the end of the freshman year in a four-year program to gain full revenue from each attrition student. That's assuming an average acquisition cost of the schools I have studied at about $5,460, plus lost potential tuition and fee revenue.

The cost really is that high and even more since the research to establish it was completed in 2006. When one factors in all aspects of acquiring a new enrollments from marketing, lead generation and development, collateral media, salaries – not just of admissions people but *all* the people who work to bring that student into the school – specialized activities, orientation and first week's events, processing applications through final class registration, publications, and so on. Most schools do not recoup their initial investment in a new student until into the second semester. So, if a student quits before then, that creates a negative revenue situation as well as probable bad debt, collection costs, and write-offs.

Putting a *Learn and Earn* approach into action is not all that difficult, but it does take a shift of focus away from assuming we *know* what students want and need to a riskier questioning of what we *really* know about our students. Let's ask them and find out if our assumptions had any validity? It is a risky approach because in academia, knowledge is power. Asking the students, the customers, to supply the knowledge thus shifts the power base away from us to them. This could cause disruption in what we do and know as correct because we always thought it was true. Not always a comfortable position for some academics.

Learn and Earn asks administrators and staff to emphasize listening and learning from the students. Rather than believe we know the answers, it becomes more important to know the right questions. The ones who can supply those are the students. Only after real information and knowledge is learned from the students should a college plan and generate an orientation for example. The same is true for the institution's money walk – its campus tour. Colleges usually make a mistake by setting up tours of the campus for potential students based on what the administrators and the planners might think they might have wanted to see if they were students. Or even worse, what they think they should show students to prove this is a solid academic school. They show the library, classrooms, labs and such, when the students on a tour usually have different interests. They have already decided the school can meet their academic standards and now want to get a sense of the real college and meet real people and professors so they can appreciate what it is like to go to school there. What they really want to learn about is very often quite different than what we think they need, so we need to learn from them.

Only when the institution has learned enough information should it move to planning and creating the customer service that is based on that acquired knowledge from the customer. The information learned from students becomes a primary operational planning tool yielding an actual strategic advantage to retain students rather than assuming we know what they need and want which leads to focusing on churning admissions and burning retentions.

The learning process is a constant one. It should not stop. The school needs to continuously survey, study and listen. We were given two ears and just one mouth for a reason.

Students should become teachers to the school on issues of what services they actually desire, need, and find lacking; not what we think they do or even should. As a result of this approach, the institution starts to plan and work in a more cooperative and inclusive mode which will engage the students more fully in their lives at the university or college. Students want to be more involved, and by asking them to help you, your request and responses to them (even if they are just a simple thank you for your assistance) will bond students to the college more strongly simply because you asked.

It is a bit like an anecdote about Benjamin Franklin I read somewhere a while back. According to the story, Franklin had to find a way to get some of his enemies to cooperate with him. One of them disliked him so much that when Franklin rose to speak, he would walk out of the room rather than listen to him. Without the cooperation of his political enemy, Franklin would not have been able to achieve a critical piece of legislation he felt was needed. Most thought it was an impossible task. But within a week, the man who always walked out was sitting with Franklin at a table working together on the document Franklin wanted his vote on. When asked how he did it, Franklin replied, "I asked for his help."

Students are not a college's enemies. (At least most of them are not, but we do turn some into antagonists by how we treat them.) Asking their help will tie them to the college even more strongly. Most everyone wants to be appreciated and asked to become a fuller member of a community. By helping, they are donating some of themselves. And as a result, they will bond into the college with a bit of themselves. Since it becomes more difficult to be upset with something you have bought into, they become more tolerant and understanding of issues that might have upset them previously.

In fact, students who work at the university even if it is only sweeping floors are the ones who will most ardently support it. Work-study for instance can be an extremely valuable retention tool if used well. The results of providing them the opportunity to perform service to the school are institutionally and personally very impressively positive. The college gains more closely bonded students. The students gain valuable experience and individual growth in areas most every mission statement claims to care about such as personal maturity and both personal and work ethics as well as social responsibility.

Moreover, it would be a wise policy to even attach some service contribution to most every scholarship or award a school provides someone. That service could be on or off campus but the on campus commitment can yield the greatest results for the institution, its retention and future donations if done well and fairly. The service components of a scholarship for instance should not be used to offset costs for employees but to increase the bonds to the institution. For example, have students work as on campus guides to help people find their way or answer questions from visitors or new students. Assign students to assist administrators, faculty or clerical workers in their jobs. Have students assist tour guides by becoming the *campus buddy* to prospective students who will then have a real person and voice to associate with the institution. Assign students to survey or gather information about the needs and real wants of other students. There are many valuable ways to involve students, to bond them to the school and learn from them while doing so.

Implementing Learn and Earn

Initially, the easiest way to explain how a school can implement *Learn and Earn* is to learn about and listen to the student and staff members. Keep in mind that staff members are very valuable points of information. They are on the front line. They encounter and work with students much more directly than an administrator or manager. They also have concerns that need to be taken into account when planning a customer service and retention strategy. In fact, we have found that staff issues often run parallel to many student issues at many schools.

For example, clerical and staff members are often not considered in decision making, and their concerns and needs are often as overlooked as those of students. This may sound a bit harsh, but it is true at far too many universities and colleges.

Consider how often staff members are asked to participate on committees as more than a recording secretary or support to the committee? How often do senior administrators meet with staff to solicit ideas and learn from them? Has the college president ever just sat down with staff to see what their needs could be? And then do something to solve them? Do you ask staff members their thoughts on a new procedure or college-wide decision even though it is highly likely they will be the ones to have to deal with the results?

Thought so.

Surveys and How to Use Them

Many colleges and schools conduct formal and informal surveys of students, staff and faculty focused on service-related issues. They believe they learn various things from them. And indeed they might if they use them better and ask larger, more open-ended questions rather than driving to a self-reinforcing question such as *On a 1-5 scale with 5 being absolutely true and 1 absolutely not - This is the best university you have attended?* Sure you get the responses that make you and your bosses and the Board of Trustees happy but what do you really learn? How will the responses help improve service and retention?

You might just ask people "If you could change one thing at this university today, what would it be?" Then group the responses into logical clusters to see if there are commonalities or themes that emerge. Next let the institution know what the top five to ten issues were. Let them also know that the college is working on at least numbers 1-3 at this time, and here is the approach. Ask everyone if they have any further thoughts on the issues. If the school wants to prove it is listening (which is always a very good idea and a key to success) solve issue number 1 before sending out the notification. If possible, rank order the issues to make number 1 an issue that can be solved quickly even if it were really lower in the count. This action demonstrates to the community that this was not your typical academic exercise that pretends to care. It is one that leads to action not to backpedaling and excuses. This is extremely important.

The remaining results could keep you busy for a long time if you try to resolve all the issues yourself. That would be a time consuming and ineffective approach that could also lead to assertions of not involving the campus community. Bring as many people into the process as will lead to action and success instead of deliberation and debating with no results other than hurt feelings. We have found that a committee or group of five attached to solving an issue can generally move forward to a conclusion and decision.

Engage the community in brainstorming solutions not just problems. The institution might wish to kick-off the process with a retreat on student and internal community customer service such as was done with solid success at the University of New Brunswick in Canada. When Susan Mesheau left a position in government to become the first Director of Student Recruitment & Integrated Marketing, then Executive Director of U First: Integrated Recruitment & Retention, another new office at the university, she realized that to succeed in meeting student enrollment goals would require a broad consensus. Mesheau knew that to build this consensus she had to go with the culture of the University which meant involving a broad base of both academic and administrative leaders. So she started with a survey of students who, although academically successful, had left the institution to determine why they did not continue their studies. She knew objective data was an important component of the academic community and would be a critically important component in convincing her colleagues about issues affecting retention.

Mesheau hired a market research firm to do the study, since this would provide some distance for her and her group and ensure a lack of bias in the findings. This also lessened the inevitable complaints that the study was not done correctly, was not up to someone's standards or invalid for one or another reason. She then presented the results as a prelude to a retreat that would focus on the conclusions and determining next steps needed to increase student retention. Not surprisingly, 72 percent of the reasons why students left were related to customer service issues. So without even having to use the phrase, we were able to focus the retreat on customer service.

The retreat led to some very positive results. The greatest one of all was buy-in from colleagues who could have chosen not to support the new office and effort Mesheau headed. Retention is not always a well understood aspect of the academic enterprise after all. And customer service (even academic customer service) can lead to an automatic rejection as an anti-academic concept foisted on the institution by corporate-minded administrators. The preliminary results for the University and its students have been impressive and heartening.

Metaphoric Surveying

Gerald Zaltman, Professor of Marketing and a Fellow in the Mind, Brain and Behavior Initiative at Harvard, writes about metaphoric surveying in his book *How Customers Think: Essential Insights into the Mind of the Market* (Harvard Business School Press, 2003):

> Metaphors can reveal cognitive processes beyond those shown in more literal language. They can also underrepresent *(sic)* or miss completely...Metaphors direct consumers' attention, influence their perceptions, enable them to make sense of what they encounter, and influence their decisions and actions. Therefore, understanding and influencing consumers' thoughts and decisions – and designing more valuable offerings for them – requires an exploration of the metaphors they use (p. 76-77).

Metaphoric surveying does not ask a respondent to gauge something from 1-10 with 10 as the highest nor rate specific issues such as the best or the worst…It calls on the respondent to think more figuratively, more imagistically, with more connotative than denotative functioning. For example, when I conduct metaphoric surveying, I might ask a group of students, "What TV show, song, or movie best resembles your experience at the college?" Then after asking a couple more metaphor-based and denotative questions, I would circle back to the earlier question and ask them why in 25 words or less. Not that I would necessarily trust the answer, but the words chosen to discuss the earlier comparison can lead to additional information on emotions, expressive somewhat subconscious appreciations of the university.

In a college in which AcademicMAPS conducted a small metaphoric survey, we asked a group of staff to choose a TV show that best represented the college. Seventy-one percent of the respondents chose *The Office.* When we announced the findings, almost all of group laughed and nodded their heads enthusiastically. When we dug a bit deeper and asked them to cast their office with that of the show if it fit, 82% chose their boss as Michael, 11% chose Dwight and the other 7% either chose another character or did not cast their boss. That told us a lot about how they perceived their bosses.

We asked them to cast themselves in the show. Fifty-four percent chose Jenna. Another nine percent chose other characters that might be closer to their particular role or level in the office (non clerical). But 37% did not see themselves in the show at all. They could not cast themselves. Could it be that 37% of the employees did not see themselves as part of the group or did not want to be part? This gave us an avenue to explore that would never have arisen without using metaphoric surveying.

The single metaphorical survey question joined with the concentrated follow-up provided many other slanting yet sincere and meaningful insights that were important. I learned the employees saw their school offices and workspaces as a somewhat pleasant place because of the camaraderie of the people they worked with but not quite a comedy. Not that many laughs per day.

They felt there was a level of incompetence in the school's leadership and, like the show, most of them just felt like extras. The show also matched many of their attitudes toward their work and the college in that they felt a level of derision and ridicule for many of the *leaders* of the school as they did for some of the characters on the show. Here we felt that was better than any anger or dislike one can develop for a character. They could and did laugh about it rather than let it cause anger at the school or its administrators. They felt the TV show did not address the unproductive and useless infighting and politics of the college that created a constant undercurrent of division and derision. After we explored the show as metaphor more felt that the fact that *The Office* was just out there to sell paper separated it finally from the college's goal of educating students and making a change in lives.

There were many other comments and ideas that came out of a close analysis of the written comments. It has become apparent that using metaphoric surveying can produce much deeper and subconsciously hidden thoughts and attitudes than the normative question-response mode.

The question-response results from 1 to 10 surveys are helpful, but too many respondents *play to the interviewer* and provide what answers they believe the surveyor is looking for. Sometimes this is because the respondents want to please the surveyor. Other times, they fear the surveyor might not like the results and there could be repercussions such as from faculty evaluations. Students realize faculty hold the power of grades over students and some believe that power remains even after they leave that person's class. Some indicate that they believe some faculty even collude to *get even* for weak evaluations. Or they may be concerned that faculty might even sue them as Dartmouth University lecturer Priya Venkatesan attempted in 2008. She was upset about the evaluations she received, so she employed the good ol' American approach: Sue students!!

Respondent bias can be especially strong in focus groups during which participants very often work hard to tell the leader what they think will be correct and impressive. Students do like to shine after all. And the focus group leader quite often telegraphs desired responses by the framing of the question. One way to help overcome the bias can be by having the focus group led by a fellow student or by using a form of metaphoric surveying. For instance, rather than use verbal responses, place a stack of a variety of magazines on a table along with scissors, paper and glue. Ask the participants a question. Then ask them to respond by picking out a picture from a magazine that best represents how they would answer. Follow that up with a discussion with each respondent and the group explaining how the picture presents their response. Let the group join in the discussion and help focus the information. Take notes and then seek correspondences from the responses to find underlying thoughts and issues. Tape the discussion if possible for later review. This is not an invitation for pop psychology. Leave that for experts who have greater experience with metaphoric survey analysis. But there will be clusters of thoughts, issues, concerns or responses that can lead to important insights that would likely not come up in more traditional focus groups or surveying.

Interviewing

It is certainly acceptable and can be helpful to conduct formal interviews or focus group sessions with students or staff. They can be helpful if one continually guards for the playing to or pleasing the interviewer. This is a significant issue during exit interviews with students. In these interviews, the student just wants to leave and do so without causing any issues or delays. So they will often tell the interviewer they are leaving for personal reasons. That will satisfy the interviewer since it does not indicate criticism of the school which the interviewer may feel compelled to defend. The student gets out faster without any need to really discuss why he or she is leaving. He or she may be telling the truth of course. Our research has found that up to 6% of all students actually do leave for personal, family, or medical reasons which could fall into the personal category. But my research finds that the typical personal issue could be phrased as, "Personally, I hate this place."

Forget about assuming they are Generation Y, or Millennial, or whatever term is in vogue. These are just broad market labeling generalizations and may not at all encompass the reality of the particular community of students at the school. For example, over 50 percent of all college students are adults, yet the labels do not even address them. Students may come from a social niche, region, or mindset that has nothing to do with any labels. Learn who they really are – not what anyone would wish them to be. Don't assume what the *experts* say about the social and communal demographics of the current students. We can generalize with accuracy about all-inclusive generations of students, but a particular college or university is not a generalization. The students who chose to attend and stay at a college form a distinctive group at that unique institution.

Use the generalizations as a touchstone perhaps but not as a statement about who any particular body of students actually is. Go to where the students are most comfortable rather than asking them to an office to talk. Talk with them in lounges, eating areas and small groups gathered in the halls. Put together some focus groups, open-meeting gripe sessions and better yet, use metaphoric survey techniques or get someone who can do this. And listen for a while before you make any decisions on who they are. It is also quite likely that it will be found there is not ***a*** student body but many parts to that body; each with its individual likes and dislikes, needs and culture or subculture.

It may turn out that there could be some general themes but also distinctive needs of different groups. Just think about the following for example. Although a college is a self-proclaimed religious Christian-oriented institution, it will be different from other schools even of the same denomination. There are many fine Methodist, Catholic, Evangelical Christian, and other religiously-oriented colleges and universities for instance. Yet they are all different from one another. Notre Dame is different from Catholic University. Southern Methodist from Clark Atlanta University. Liberty College is distinct from Oral Roberts. And Brigham Young is unlike any of the others. Making a generalization about them all would lead to some quite inaccurate assumptions in most every case. Even within each institution there will be variations. Every student is an individual and will associate with like-minded students forming small groups with their own spiritual personas. Every religious subgroup on campus will have different needs and concerns that will be different even within the larger convergence points of agreement.

Colleges that really learn about and from their students and do not work from assumptions about them will succeed by providing relevant education, good customer service, and the ultimate student goal by having companies and professions that will hire and accept their graduates. These schools use what they have learned to assure student satisfaction.

Don't Believe Tink!

Remember the scene in the Mary Martin version of *Peter Pan* when Tinkerbell is dying because we may not believe in her enough? And Peter turns to us and says "Please believe. Tell Tink you believe!" And we do. Well, maybe more of us need to leave that belief in the theater and not apply it in customer service issues in college.

Generally, it appears too many colleges use a set of beliefs and not facts to form their understanding and thoughts about their students' knowledge of how the college works as well as how to navigate through it. There are so many assumptions made about the students, their abilities and understandings of what we all know as our college, its rules, and folkways. We assume they will somehow know them too. After all, we do, and aren't we all at college together?

Unfortunately, the answer is no. They do not know, and we must supply the directions. Having had experience with public educational structures and systems does not mean they know how to be intelligent, competent users of a college. They need clear user instructions not just on the academic and administrative regulations but on everything starting with how to get from the dorm to their classes or to the administrative offices. Just as when you first moved to an area and everyone assumed you knew how to get around. "Sure, the super market. Well, just go down 104. Take a left at State Road 5. It isn't marked like that but you'll know it when you see it. And when you see the Catholic Church, take a left. Now the Catholic Church is near the Last Evangelical so don't be fooled. If you miss the Catholic Church, you'll know it because you'll soon come up on the Jewish synagogue. It's just after Dave's on the right. Good hamburgers there by the way. Good luck."

Uhh, how do I get to 104?
Good customer service demands that the customer, the student, knows how to use the services provided and required. Ever tried to assemble a gift or use new software that had poor or almost nonexistent directions with parts and abbreviations that the technician knew but did not explain to you? Sure you have used an outdoor grill or HTML based webs, but that does not mean you know how to put a grill together or use web site building language. The result? If you were not afraid to look stupid, you asked for help. If not, the grill was returned and the software not used. In any case, you likely became frustrated and angry and swore off, or at, the manufacturer.

Students are no different except they are even more tentative than you or I, and they may not ask for help. They do not want to look stupid after all. They will become aggravated, angry and blame the college thus becoming a potential attrition statistic.

And navigating academic rules? Forget it. Just give it up. Most students plagiarize because they do not know what it really is nor do they understand it is not acceptable. The web is an anonymous research tool so anything there is available for the copying. Moreover, they have, after all, grown up in the Doris Kearns Goodwin/Laurence Tribe/Stephen Ambrose period. The one in which it is okay for some to plagiarize but not others.

Add/drop? Not done at many schools simply because the students are not made aware of the process. Financial problems? A bursar informed me recently students generally are not fully made aware of what all the acronyms mean – FAFSA, Pell, Stafford, and the bursar's office is too busy to explain to "people who should know".

But why don't they know all this? Partially because of the Tinkerbell Theory.

The Tinkerbell Theory is most clearly elucidated in the belief colleges have that their students know how to be students. Actually, too many schools have a misguided belief in Peter Pan and fairy dust. They believe that somehow magic occurs on the stage in the local school auditorium at high school graduation. An immature high schooler starts across the stage, and with him or her walks all the ways of thinking and attitudes ingrained over 12 long years. These are the same very characteristics that made the soon-to-be high school graduate have to prove he or she was capable of succeeding in your college. Then, he or she stops and just as the high school principal hands over a diploma, a small, invisible maturity fairy flies overhead and sprinkles magic knowledge dust on the graduate. POOF!! You're a college freshman! What was a latent college student suddenly sheds his or her immature ways and is suddenly metamorphosed into a mature college student ready and capable of meeting the demands and dictates of college!

And if for some odd reason the fairy dust did not complete the transformation, the next ten weeks of summer vacation complete the transformation. After all, that freshman is no longer a high schooler. He or she is a freshman at Neverland U and all our students know how to be students. After all, they are here at college.

But this is far from the truth. Peter Pan was fictional and so is the belief that incoming students are college students upon walking on campus.

It is important that colleges educate their students on how they are to be students. How they can become intelligent users of the college. It is not enough to give someone a catalog. A college I work with recently found out from its State authorities that simply because something is in the catalog does not make it automatically qualify as fully informing students. The school believed that if it was printed in there, it was law. Not so said the State. The college had an active obligation to make sure the students were fully aware of the school's rule. Even worse, the upset students were even stronger in their frustration over a lack of understanding of the rule in question. The State informed the college it was wrong. That led to contrition. Some students became angry and that led to attrition.

Another college posted its dates for registration for the next semester on its student website. Then the school was very upset when some students did not show to register. The college officials believed the students should have known from the website. But they did not instruct students clearly enough on how to get a password, the how to navigate the site and finally the need to check the front page on a regular basis. Besides, the reality was, and is for most all schools, students do not use the portal and if they do, they do not use it as the college or university intended. Students at the college thought the site was just for getting their final grades, checking their bills and other administrative bothers. They were not aware they needed to check it for announcements.

Besides, in high school if they missed a registration date, or even an assignment, they just did it late. No penalty. How would they know the rules were different at the institution if the college did not inform them?

Who is to blame? Not the customer. It was the provider who assumed that everyone knew how to use a website, had a computer and went to the college portal. But that is not a safe assumption. Not every student has that knowledge, and if they do it may be about Yahoo or Google, not your college (which, believe it or not, will lose out to their own email, IM and gaming sites). Moreover, we have found that your college or university portal is not where students start their hours of web browsing every day. The college portal loses almost every time if the student is using his or her own computer.

A major problem in the appropriate use – and thus the effectiveness of a service or product – is that it is supposed the user will understand how to use it or do something because I do. Do not assume the students of a college will understand the institution's assembly and operation instructions simply because you know them or have them and may have printed them in a flier or brochure. If you believe something is important, it must be explained and made clear if students are to be able to use the college correctly.

Good customer service calls on the service provider to vigorously and aggressively educate the recipient and/or user of the services on the proper use and operation of the services. Tell them once.

Then tell them again, and finally tell them you just told them. Then make sure they heard you.

Create a user guide for students. Put it together as if you are telling someone how to assemble a toy or piece of Ikea furniture. For dropping a course for example, it could start with:

1. **Determine if this is a course you can drop**
   a. Is it a required course in your curriculum?
   b. Are the skills and knowledge from the course needed in those that follow it?
   c. Can it be taken out of sequence?
   Note: If a, or b is answered yes, reconsider dropping the course.
2. **Do you have an add drop form?**
   a. If no go to ______ or get one online at ______________.
3. **Complete the add drop form. Be certain**
   a. The course to be dropped is correct and has the correct course code
   b. If adding a course, be certain it has the correct course code and the new course fits in your remaining schedule
4. **Obtain any and all required permission signatures**
   a. To drop: faculty of the course being dropped
   b. To add: faculty accepting you in the new course
5. **File the add drop form with the _________ office by (date)**
6. **Check with the business office for any adjustments that will have to be made in your tuition and fees.**

This is an example, of course. The exact steps at a particular institution may well be different. If so, the How to Drop information will have to be changed to reflect the actual procedure.

This format can be used for almost any administrative or other action students may have to take. Determine what students are doing incorrectly or to their detriment, and create a How to Guide for that situation. Then make certain every student gets the information. One way to do that is to be certain to review it at orientation and information sessions. The information can also be effectively distributed by sliding sheets under dorm doors and hang them in the bathrooms above or in the stalls. Also leave stacks in the entrance area to the bathrooms. Students will read them there.

And to be safe, don't believe Tink. Do the same for administrative, faculty and staff bathrooms. It always amazes me and others how much we do not know about our own schools.

Required Attendance is Good Service

Customer service is in no way equal to pandering to students. Though I often hear academics, mainly faculty, say they believe customer service will just mean giving students easy grades. That is very far from what real service is. In fact, giving easy grades would clearly be a disservice to students, to the school and to the integrity of everyone. Moreover, easy grades are not what most students want even though they will accept them in classes they do not judge as core to their future success.

Students come to higher education institutions to become prepared for a future job and career. That requires us to give them the best service we can to fulfill our obligation. Not to lie or mislead our students with grades they do not earn. Just as we would never knowingly provide students incorrect information, knowledge or skills, neither should we provide them education, training or grades they do not require or deserve.

I'll say it again, customer service is not pandering or simply smiling or pretending the customer is always right. As we have already discussed – they aren't. And here is another example of when customers are wrong and we can be too depending on how we do things.

Considering that students go to school to *become* something and get a job, part of the service we need to provide them is not just knowledge and skill training but also job prep. This includes not merely preparing them to just get a job but to keep it. It is critically important that colleges teach students professional as well as people and social skills to retain them. And no, job preparation and professionalism do not go against the mission and values of the academia or the liberal arts. In fact it should be argued that they can add to both by helping students appreciate each more.

As a card carrying liberal artist, I can attest to the reality that our goals are to interest and prepare students to enter liberal arts areas and activities like teaching literature, working in some liberal arts-related area. We can proclaim that our goal is not to prepare students for jobs but for knowledge, but as we attempt to entice students into our areas of study, we are working to get them to enter a field of study and work. The same rules will apply for them in their work as it will for any one. Actually, most of liberal arts majors will end up going into jobs like sales and entry-level management that will have the same or similar requirements for those students who majored in business, engineering, medicine or any other endeavor. And if they go on for a master's or even a PhD, they will have requirements that come with their job such as completing assignments, due dates, research, and appointments they have to attend at a given time, for example.

So what is involved with career prep? One aspect of this is teaching students to be responsible employees and individuals so they can keep the jobs they get. That is done by making them responsible students who earn what grades they achieve. To begin with, we review the important quote of that major media corporate guru and film maker **Allan** Stewart Konigsberg (Woody Allan). "Ninety-seven percent of life is showing up." And that is a keen summary of a major issue for employers but they also add *on time*. That's the first lesson on career prep, which will also have a very strong positive impact on a college's retention. Having students learn to show up for class and on time. That's right! Attendance.

If your school does not have an attendance policy, it is making a significant error. First, it is failing to provide a specifically important job skill. Employers do not leave it up to employees to decide if they want to come to work or not. It is not a personal choice. It is a work requirement. If an employee misses a day or two of work without valid reason, he or she doesn't simply lose half a grade. He or she loses a job!

So to really serve our clients, we should require attendance to help prepare them for life. A wonderful byproduct of requiring this customer service is an increase in retention in both classes and the school.

When a school or a faculty member tells students it is not necessary to attend classes, it is also a statement that what goes on in class has no value. If a student can pass a course without being in class to hear the lectures, see how the problems are solved, learn from the faculty member, then that reality is a strong decree that the classes and faculty member have nothing to offer. Nothing.

Besides, what does it say to students when a faculty member says you can pass my course without coming to class? It says *I have nothing to offer you. I can be replaced by the text books. And if you can pass the course without my help, you certainly do not need me. I have no education value to you.*

What self-respecting faculty member, what professional would want to stand before a room of clients and offer that up? Yet, some professors do that regularly. They will allow students to skip class and still be able to pass the course. It reflects poorly on colleagues as well as the individual instructor. Telling students they can succeed without the faculty degrades every other faculty member who takes his or her teaching responsibilities and professional self seriously.

As Einstein is reported to have said "Education is what is left after we forget all the facts and dates." It is education that really prepares us to become a functioning member of a society and culture. Some of the lessons of education are not learned by books but through the everyday lessons we provide students through our actions, standards and comportment. Students need to value their education, as well as their learning, skill attainment and career prep. But when we do not value classroom learning and demand attendance, what we do is devalue the core of the academic enterprise itself. By extension, those who allow students to not attend and do well anyhow demean the value and integrity of the whole college. Their inaction says the learning experience itself can be without value. If that is so, then why stay?

Granted, lack of an attendance policy is not the only factor for a student to drop out or transfer from a school. But it is one of the most significant contributors for many. How do I know? Every school that we have worked with to implement an attendance policy has increased retention the very first semester the policy was put in place.

Customer Service and Fund Raising

While speaking with a group of university advancement and development professionals, a simple yet very important epiphany about retention came into my head. It was a realization so obvious and important to these professionals that it was surprising they were not leading proponents of retention at their institutions. Here it is:

STUDENTS WHO DROP OUT OF YOUR SCHOOL, NEVER BECOME ALUMNI!

Thus, schools lose on all three ends of the potential continuum when students drop out. Students lose their chance at a better life from the education they would have received at your school. Tuition revenue is lost. Potential donations are lost. That makes the advancement peoples' job that much harder. Fewer alumni equals fewer donation sources. And considering that a major role of presidents today is raising money and alumni are a major source of donations, attrition can make the attainment of success that much more arduous.

A university or college can use alumni giving percentage as a metric to gauge their customer service. People give to organizations like colleges that they like, and that make them feel good. The liking aspect is directly linked to how the college treated the alumni when they were students. If the school fulfilled the three ROI's (financial, emotional and affective), there is a higher likelihood that graduates will donate as alumni. If the school made the experience feel like a four- to six-year root canal, odds are extremely high alumni will not donate. So, one way you can gauge how well you serve students and make their experience a positive one is looking at the percentage of alumni giving at the institution.

These alumni participation metrics can be even more precise indicators if they can be linked back to specific majors, work areas, events, etc. If a particular work area has a very low internal level of donations, that is a spot that needs greater attention and increased customer service to increase morale and engagement with the institution. If students graduating from a particular major have a lower participation rate then other majors, that could be an indicator of a service problem in that area. Of course, if it is a major like art or philosophy, you will need to factor in the potentially lower discretionary money of these graduates. Less income leads to less money to give to the school.

The metric also works for employees and how they feel they are served by the university. You can evaluate the morale of and service to the internal community by the percentage of internal participation in a university's fund raising effort. The lower the percentage, the lower the morale and feeling of positive engagement levels. And considering that most schools have a less than optimal internal give rate and an increasing employee turnover rate…well, let's just say that there is room to improve.

But again, all these alumni indices and metrics do not matter if students do not graduate. And employees who quit generally do not wish to donate either.

Happier Students and Faculty

Attitude Comes to College

Social critics and we in higher education have found the general lack of civility in our culture also exists on our campuses. This should be no surprise. The people who live in our *Happy Bunny* "It's all about me" culture are our students and our employees. They are our faculty, administrators and lo and behold, they are also us.

As Walt Kelly had his cartoon character Pogo put it so well back in the 60's: *We have met the enemy, and they are us.* The people who attend and work at our schools are the exact same people in the exact same culture we think we have left behind when we enter the retreat for intellectual and academic pursuit we know as a college campus. But what we find is that what attitudes apply in the so-called real world outside of academia also apply on a college campus.

This reality can also explain differences in the ways we perceive and act toward one another. Our students come from a cultural group that has been immersed in a cynical, smart mouth me first attitude which has eliminated most of what older America grew up knowing as social civilities and courtesies. The Captain Kangaroo/Mister Rogers world of please, thank you and general polite regard for one another has been replaced by a hip-hop attitude that revels and condones a general rude incivility toward one another. Radio shock jocks use language and casually discuss topics on the radio some of our generation may well be taken aback by and even find anti-intellectual or uncivil. Language that might have been thought of as anti-social and rebellious is now everyday colloquial use in casual discussion even in classrooms and offices. Attitudes that would have been unacceptable and considered rude such as taking a phone call in class or napping during lectures have become the norm according to many faculty members.

Our parents and their parents and theirs all the way back to Young Socrates in the Platonic dialogues had difficulty understanding and accepting the current younger generation's music, hair, language, attitudes, mores and actions. Each generation knew the student group was more out of control than the last.

Or as Paul Lind put it for our parents and grandparents about us in *Bye Bye Birdy*

> Kids!
> I don't know what's wrong with these kids today!
> Kids!
> Who can understand anything they say?
> Kids!
> They are so ridiculous and immature!
> Kids!
> I don't see why anybody wants 'em!
> Kids!
> They are just impossible to control!
> Why can't they be like we were, perfect in every way?
> Oh, what's the matter with kids today?

Actually, there is a difference in kids today. More than in the past perhaps, and that is causing some service clashes on campus. We, the boomer and yuppie generations, taught them too well. We encouraged them to take the next step in being more rebellious, more anti-authority, discourteous, disrespectful and become self-centered, demanding. In a large sense, we created the college students we encounter. Our generations rebelled against authority and carried that forward by replacing much of the processes of etiquette with a sense of privilege for the next generations. They were taught that they *are as good as anyone else. You can be anything you wish to be. Don't let anyone tell you no. Age is not necessarily an indicator that a person warrants politeness or respect.* On the one hand, students were inculcated with a media and marketing liturgy of their importance in the quest for class-free equality. The motto, "Don't trust anyone over thirty" has continued, though the age threshold has dropped to anyone older than oneself. We also turned them into cultural and consumer cynics as we taught them not to trust advertising, marketing or promotional media. Unfortunately for colleges, that cynicism does extend to the marketing they do. As a result, we created the consumer mentality we now find so offensive when a student tells us, "Hey, I'm paying for your salary."

Additionally, technology has allowed the members of the current college student generation to isolate themselves from the larger community thereby greatly reducing the many social and face-to-face interactions one needs to learn social and cultural mores, codes and folkways. The Educause Center for Applied Research reported in 2008 that 80.3 percent of college students report using social networking sites regularly, up from 72.3% in 2006. The social networking sites are also the most used of all sites on the web attracting the largest amount of the average 16 hours of web browsing and usage per week. The social networks of YouTube, My Space, Hi5, Facebook and Friendster, chat rooms, and download pirating networks like The Pirate Bay and Mininova allow students to be in a *community* without any need to ever be with someone physically. These communities have different mores, traditions, codes as well as greater tolerance for negative or boorish behavior than the analog world of higher education found on the campuses of colleges, universities or even career colleges where behavioral codes can be a bit more lenient. Emails also permit the student generation to communicate with others without ever having to deal with live, face-to-face interaction.

As a result, they learn social codes that can tolerate anti-social behavior such as *flaming*. Wikipedia defines flaming as

> The hostile and insulting interaction between Internet users. Flaming usually occurs in the social context of a discussion board, Internet Relay Chat (IRC) or even through e-mail. An Internet user typically generates a flame response to other posts or users posting on a site, and such a response is usually not constructive, does not clarify a discussion, and does not persuade others. Sometimes, flamers attempt to assert their authority, or establish a position of superiority over

> other users. Other times, a flamer is simply an individual who believes he or she carries the only valid opinion. This leads him or her to personally attack those who disagree.

Flaming is not always tolerated on all websites or networks but it is common enough to be found on most interactive or participatory sites. Moreover, people can feel quite at ease with full freedom to flame without concern for retaliation since they can hide behind a user name or the oft used moniker *anonymous* that does not directly identify them in analog life. As a result of this anonymity flaming, bullying and an assertive nastiness that would not be well tolerated in a real face-to-face social interaction can be common. Furthermore, a communication problem can arise for student communicators when after either participating in or reading enough flaming messages the aggressive and mostly anonymous communication behavior transfers into real life interactions. Students do not necessarily learn or acquire the socialization needed to learn in person interpersonal skills. This lack of social communication skill development certainly limits them with the normative variations in successful inter-generational interactions. This can account for some of the clashes found in working with uneducated communicators and even trying to assist them on campus. Students with weak communication skills just may not know how to communicate appropriately with campus community members of a different age and role.

Technology is only one contributing factor that has blurred the distinctions between what the sociologist Erving Goffman described so well as front and back stage performances in his classic book *Presentation of Self in Everyday Life.* (1967) Goffman describes the social world of communication events as happening as if they were on a performance stage of a society. He divides the stage into its two major locations of front stage and back stage. As in a play, front stage is where the actors perform their formal roles. They are aware they are being observed and judged by the audience so they play the proscribed part. In society, front stage performers are aware they are being observed and thus perform using socially and culturally proscribed roles and language acceptable to the role they are playing and to the audience listening to it. For example, when a faculty member steps before a class to lecture, he or she does so using tone, language, gestures and such that would be far different than when he or she is explaining how the day went to a spouse. He or she would use a very different tone, language and performance values when telling a child the same information just told to the spouse. The performance would be appropriate to the role and audience.

Back stage communications occur when the actors are off stage, behind the curtains so they cannot be seen by the audience. They can be more of their so-called natural selves as opposed to playing a specific part in the play. Their language does not have to be that used in front of the audience for example. Granted they are, as Goffman notes, playing the role of a person in a play but not on stage at the moment. As a result, they are under less pressure to perform in a particular approved manner or speak specific lines appropriate to their formal performance role. Behind the curtains, they can be more relaxed and speak and act in a more relaxed manner if they wish.

Front stage social roles place pressure on the people involved to perform their roles appropriate to the interaction of the situation, the audience and social norms. If a young person is talking with a priest for example, there are normally restraints placed on the use of language, tone and attitude. If the actors realize they are involved in a front stage performance, the interaction is one that most academics have come to believe should be similar to that of a student interacting with them. But if a person does not realize that he or she is in a front stage performance or has not learned normative social interaction behaviors called upon for the role, there will be a resultant clash between the expected and the actual.

For many students today, the separation between front and back stage has eroded. Students have not been taught the front stage social roles that many academics desire and expect. Whereas academics expect some level of respect for their positions and/or titles, students do not show much deference to either. For instance, just because someone has the designation of Doctor attached to the front of his or her name does not impress students much. Your being a PhD does not place much front stage pressure on students to conform to behavioral models including an automatic show of respect for our educational labels. This is a learned indifference that we have some responsibility for by the way.

When educational attire went from suits, shirts and ties for men and dresses for female teachers, this shift in costume signaled a change in the way students were to address educators. The formal attire was a sign that the teachers were playing a formal role. It stated that we are dressed this way to signal to you that we are in our official front stage roles, and you should be too. Just as a costume change in a play lets the audience knows that the character is in a different mood or role so the shift from formal to informal attire sent a message to the audience – students.

The change to more informal, more relaxed (how one might away from the classroom) back stage type of attire was a clear statement that the roles had shifted. The attempt to forge a less formal and more relaxed atmosphere worked. Perhaps too well, because it also took away the pressures to perform in socially prescribed front stage roles. That carried over to higher education where the dress can be even more back stage than in K-12. Over time, the informal roles helped erase the academic lines between front and back stage roles. As a result, many of their communications with faculty and others on a campus are back stage behaviors which are similar to those they might use with friends. The college personnel might be using more front stage communication modes, so there will inevitably be a clash which will be interpreted by the college member as a lack of respect when it is a lack of communication alignment.

If one realizes that what is occurring is a clash of front and back stage expectations, it may become easier to deal with the clash. If one can understand the clash of communicating modes not a statement of disrespect but what it really is – the variance in communication styles between generations – it should also be easier to predict the clash and it is hoped, not be taken aback by it nor simply believe the student is not being respectful and not deserving of one's attention and help.

Overcoming the Communication Clash

I would suggest that technology has also blurred the front- and back stage performances.

Emailing, text messaging, YouTube, etc. have also moved what was a back stage performance into front stage realities. Students live online in a very front stage role but do so through back stage behavior. What is a very front stage performance is somehow accepted as private communication available to millions of viewers. The web has allowed everyone to invent a persona to represent a front stage personality even though the created persona may have no reality. Students are very aware that every act of communication can become a broadcast to the world. A private email or photo can become the next new thing to move around the cyber world without the original communicator even being aware of it. Most all back stage communication has become potentially front stage.

Students and others post what one might have believed to be private information, pictures and details about oneself that melds the front and back stage distinctions almost completely. People post intimate and quite personal information that would at one time not have been even considered in the front stage world of social sanction and demand. Some of what is posted seems to be done so with a belief that the web offers full immunity from social or cultural sanctions from nude pictures of oneself, to videos of heavy drinking to even posts of movies in which illegal acts are performed.

In so doing, technology has blurred the distinctions not just between the front and back stage but between what is socially and privately proper. As a result, front stage performances now are made as if the people in them are back stage; as if they were not surrounded by millions of eyes all over the world.

The cell phone has done some of the same, too. Just think back to the last cell phone conversation you were not either speaker or listener in but had little choice but listen to. People, especially students, speak on cell phones about quite private things and acts as if they were in a room by themselves though their voices are loud enough to assure everyone in the area can (or is forced) to overhear their communication performance. The sense of privacy that many academics cherish is not necessarily shared by their students.

It may be proposed that technologies have not just blurred front and back stage but the notions of privacy and decorum as well. The division between the two often is ignored. The result is often a clash of cultures and acceptable modes of interaction between student and college staff, administrators, and faculty. The office, for example, would be seen as a locale for front stage roles of student and college administrator or staff. That would imply to the college employee a level of performance language, attitudes and tones that ought to be employed. But students with their blurred front and back stage distinctions may not play the role expected. Their attitude, tone and language choice may not fit into the expected role and performance. It may well seem and actually be that they are performing a belligerent or at least less respectful character than is appropriate to the person in the office. The result is a collision of expectations, language and attitudes that produce misunderstanding, frustration and anomie. These in turn generate the negative feelings which may dissuade people from wanting to help students.

We may not talk the same language or use the same tone and attitude in our communications with one another. This conflict is at the root of many of the problems college employees have in trying to assist students. The student has not learned to discriminate communication mode and attitude to different audiences. Students may not be conscious of or even intentional when they use an inappropriate tone with college staff, administrators or faculty. They may not even be aware they are being insulting or rude when using a petulant or aggressive attitude in a communication, because they do not learn to discriminate tone, attitude or language in social interactions. It is closer to having evolved (or devolved) into one interaction mode fits all communications which can generate communication dissonance.

It is the role of the college personnel to realize this reality and work with students to educate them to be able to develop different personas for different audiences. It is not productive, nor is it healthy to simply become defensive or upset at what might be perceived as a slight or a bad-mannered or disrespectful student. To do so would be not just poor customer service but will only reassure the student that he or she was right, and we are wrong. It would also assure that college employees leave their offices and jobs every day feeling unhappy, dissatisfied and stressed out.

It may not be easy to do, but it is important that all institutional staff learn to smile and use the old method of counting to ten or twenty if needed to overcome the initial instinct to give in to the fight or flight response.

Expect that students will be discourteous, and you can better control the immediate desire to respond in kind. Also, by expecting students to not always communicate well you create a more positive self-fulfilling prophecy that allows you to remain in control of your own behavior. Besides not all students are rude nor communicate with an attitude. So if you prepare yourself to accept and pleasantly work with those that do, you will be doubly pleased and delighted by those who communicate as we would want all the students to communicate.

Happier Teachers = More Learning

Though most faculty and some administrator deride customer service as a noxious import from business, it has been found that faculty who provide increased levels of customer service will have a better and more satisfying teaching experience. And their students will learn better with greater desire, compliance and increased retention.

When students believe a faculty member provides them good service and cares about them, they are more willing to listen and learn. Students are also more compliant with the teacher's instruction, more willing to engage in class discussions, take more notes and will complete assignments more readily. Bottom line – faculty can teach and students will learn, each with greater success.

I recall a master teacher and academic customer service provider named Dr. Taffee Tanimoto at the University of Massachusetts in Boston back in 1969. Dr. Tanimoto was the chair of the math department. He loved math and was always bothered when we students had problems with algebra. He also loved teaching. Our diffidence bordering on hostility toward math baffled him, and he admitted it in class. He also said that he might not make us become mathematicians, but he would do all he could to have us learn algebra and maybe even like some of it if we would just work with him.

To back it up, he started 7:30 to 9:00 a.m. tutoring classes that met every Tuesday and Thursday. He lived over 30 miles away from the University and took the train in to be in the classroom by 7 if any of us wanted to show up early. He would also be available in his office until 5:30 every day to go over problems with any student who needed help – even if they were not in his class. He even tutored me once at the Back Bay train station over coffee as we both waited for trains. He was patient but did not pander – no physics for poets type of classes. Full bodied algebra, calculus and trigonometry. He demanded but did not reprimand. He provided excellent, extremely important and supportive customer service that made us want to learn algebra. And we did succeed and as he said, he succeeded. I even got a C+, but even more I learned to like math even if it didn't always like me. I also grew to love the University because of the customer service I was given in the classroom but perhaps even more out of the classroom.

Customer service helped me and a group of math clods pass algebra. And it helped. Dr. Tanimoto and many other faculty like their jobs in the classroom much more than others who saw teaching as just a job, a way to make a living or study their favorite subject away from the classroom.

The customer service to willingness to learn equation is supported not only by the Taffee Tanimotos of academia whose innate drive to educate and provide service engages students by providing learning and success. It can be inculcated in others who may need to be taught some of the underlying principles and techniques of service. Realize some faculty and others may not embrace customer service as something they can personally welcome wholeheartedly. They may have to fake it, but that is okay. Just as smiling may not come naturally to some, so they would have to put on a false smile as they walked the halls and encountered students as colleagues.

A story covers this situation. There was a very grouchy and mean man in Poland who fell in love with the daughter of a gentle and kind man. The grouch was very rich and always treated others as if they were below him. When he asked for the hand of the beautiful young woman, the father said he would never let his daughter marry such a rude and grouchy man who treated others poorly. The rich man was smitten, so he decided that he would pretend to be nice and help people just until he could get married to the young woman. He began to smile and be polite. He gave charity and aided those who needed help. This he kept up until the father relented. He had to keep it up until the wedding itself. He did so. Then as soon as the ceremony was over, a poor man asked him for a kopek. Without thinking, the rich man gave him two kopek. He tried to be mean but he had faked being nice so long that he had become a nice man, and he found it made him happy as well as his new wife. So if people on campus have to fake what they learn from customer service workshops or training, that is okay. The results will still be the same.

This has been learned from the reports of colleges and universities that have engaged faculty in customer service training. There are other formal academic studies and reports that help forward this position. Two studies, the *2006 National Survey of Student Engagement (NSSE)* and another by Hombury, Koschate and Hoyer in the April 2005 issue of the *Journal of Marketing* on customer service and willingness to pay (WTP) alongside consideration of interactional equity theory, support our contentions with their research.

In the 2006 NSSE Director's Report the following is stated:

> For years, researchers have pointed to involvement in educationally purposeful activities as the gateway to desired outcomes of college. Students who engage more frequently in educationally effective practices get better grades, are more satisfied, and are more likely to persist. Two decades ago, this literature prompted Chickering, Gamson and their colleagues to compile a list of "Seven Principles for Good Practice in Undergraduate Education," which are reflected in many NSSE survey items. Recent findings from independent studies have corroborated the relationships between engagement and indicators of student success in college such as grades and persistence with undergraduates in different types of institutional settings. These studies also show that while engagement is positively linked to desired outcomes for all types of students, historically underserved students tend to benefit more than majority students (p.10).

We have no disagreement with this observation. Instead we add that the same is true for faculty when they become engaged with their students. Moreover, we add that though there is no disagreement with the NSSE panel's recommendations of curricula and pedagogy they feel would add to engagement, true engagement comes from appropriate customer services to students.

The TV show Cheers can provide an excellent example of this. This was a show about a community of barflies who were – to be very honest – a group of losers. They seemed to have little value or meaning outside of that bar. It was in Cheers that they became important, and they each returned the commitment.

When Norm, a perennially out of work, not all that attractive, fat, nobody in the world outside of Cheers entered the bar he was embraced and became important. In Cheers, everyone knew his name and made it clear that they were glad he came. Each and every time he walked into the bar, the entire community would yell out, "Norm." That act of calling out his name provided him value, meaning and even a bit of celebrity. As a result, Norm felt important and would never abandon Cheers even when he could easily gone to Gary's Olde Time Tavern which always beat Cheers in all competitions, had a bigger TV and better service and clientele. He could not think of leaving Cheers because it proved its engagement in him every time. This was true engagement.

It is important to note that Cheers took the first step. It reached out to Norm, knew his name and cared about him as a person. That made him engage in Cheers. In the same way, colleges and universities need to extend themselves to their clients and customers before they will engage in it.

Service makes a student believe he is important enough for the school to care about him, so he will reach back and find a place within it and the education it can provide. If a student believes the college, the faculty and staff care about her, she will return that emotional investment. This is the type of engagement that must be created before pedagogical or curricula engagement can be achieved. If students feel that no one knows their name, i.e. no one cares about them, they are much less likely to engage with curriculum or pedagogy or stay at the college.

Greater Classroom and Teaching Fulfillment/Pleasure

Increased customer service also yields greater faculty fulfillment and enjoyment in the classroom. Certainly a much sought after prize. There is a direct correlation between customer service and the resulting student/faculty engagement that leads to willingness to learn (WTL). This correlation also controls instructional satisfaction for faculty and leads directly to improvements in morale and appreciation of both students and the institution itself. If students are willing (even wanting) to learn, it makes the teaching job that much easier and more enjoyable. Keep in mind that people do not want to disappoint those they like and respect. So engaged students will work with faculty so they can succeed in teaching more if the faculty treat them with good customer and service equity as a start.

Willingness to learn and willingness to engage (WTE) are extremely important now with the ever growing number of adjuncts. Adjuncts are not necessarily that attached to a school that lets him/her know they are expendable and not highly valued (low pay, no benefits and a constantly uncertain future can do that). The school does not really create an engagement for adjuncts, so their engagement must come from the classroom itself. If the students are not that engaged with the adjunct, there will be a rift that interferes with student learning, attachment to the class and the school and that leads to increased attrition.

Schools should spend time helping teachers teach from a genuine customer service base. Easy grades do not make faculty well liked but as Good Academic Customer Principle 13 directs:

> Do not cheapen the product and call it customer service.
> No pandering.

What will engage students are faculty who are fair and demanding and are not afraid to let students see these qualities in their teaching and grading.

Easy Grades are Not Customer Service

Limited or easy readings, assignments or tests are not customer service and students know it. As Baskin Robbins says "Anyone Can Make a Cheaper Product". To this I add, *that does not mean that customers will really like it better either.* Chocolate chip ice cream with one chip is not chocolate chip no matter how cheap it is. And an A is not an A if nothing is really learned. Giving a high grade when not deserved or little has been accomplished is merely pandering to an incorrect assumption of what students want and cheating the customer. Teaching did not take place, and the customer did not get what he or she paid for. Remember always that the ultimate aspect on which true customer service value rests is if the customer gets what he or she is paying for. If the service is great at a restaurant and the food is not good, a waiter will not bring you back.

Students may not refuse an easy course or a higher grade than deserved but they do not respect it, the teacher, the class or the school. And if it is a course they believe they will need in their career, watch out. They in fact feel their education is being cheapened and will look elsewhere since their education means their future and career. The latest CIRP/HERI report out of UCLA shows that the trend toward seeing college as a way to a good career and personal wealth continues to grow in importance. It has always been a major motivational factor for attending and graduating college, by the way. Even we administrators and faculty took courses we did not want to take, maybe even hated, as a vocational necessity.

We took them because we were in school to become a professor so we could then profess that college should be for something other than getting a job, for becoming something. We from the boomers generation really thought the same, but we had been trained to couch our material goals in a veneer of wanting to learn and grow as an individual. Just as any of the millionaire hippy capitalists who started in a head shop.
Creating happier teachers and students can be accomplished fairly easily with just a bit of awareness of the value of customer service and some training in simple and academically appropriate practices such as making attendance important, showing one cares about student learning and about their becoming socially and culturally educated and techniques like *give a name/get a name.*

Service Equity and Faculty Classroom Pleasure at Cheers University

Know Their Names

A basic aspect of customer service in colleges is the creation of service equity between the customer and the school, its personnel and certainly the faculty. Service equity then resides in the perception that the college and faculty put as much effort into the relationship as an individual student does. If students perceive a level of service equity in the way they and the faculty interrelate such as through the *give a name/get a name* technique, there is a corresponding increase in willingness to learn (WTL).

Faculty often present their names in large, hard to read chalk letters the first day of class so students can see they are open and friendly, "Hi call me Dr. Professor Fred, PhD", but as often they make little effort to learn the students' names. There is not much social equity shown in that.

Learn who they are. If your memory for names is not all that great, set up a seating chart. You can even tell students you are doing this so you can learn their names because they are important individuals. Then get rid of the chart as soon as you do so. It's also okay to admit your memory for names is not as great, but it is important that you get to know each of them as individuals. Look at the list. Use it to call on students by name. First names! Not last names unless you teach at a British boarding school in the 1920's.

Names create engagement and shared sense of value. The result will be that students will comply more eagerly and more fully with professors' assignments, rules and lectures, that is, they will engage. Faculty will have students who are more involved in class, more compliant with their instructions and requirements, and more engaged in their studies if faculty know their students' names. It shows not just sharing but also respect.

Be Glad They Came

Make the students feel as if you want to teach them; as if you are happy they came to your class. Indeed all faculty should be. After all though the dumb adage goes "This would be a great place to work if it weren't for the students", there would not be a college if there were no students.

It should be seen as an honor for students to choose your class or as an almost equal honor if they are assigned. You've been given the chance to really make a difference in their lives through your teaching. If a faculty member does not feel this honor, this opportunity to help students grow and become stronger intellectually and personally, one should find out what the heck he or she is doing teaching.

Faculty should develop and show recognition that the students are valued and important. Students should never feel as if the faculty member looks down on them. The mean, austere, demeaning dictatorial teacher might be good for movies but not for classrooms. Students want to feel as if the faculty wants to reach them and will work as hard as they will with respect given and expected. In more technical terms, they expect and demand a sense of service equity.

If faculty feel they should have better students in their classes to teach, they have it wrong. The goal should be to do all you can to make the students better. That is really the job of teaching anyhow.

Learn to like the students you have and enjoy life more. The students will learn more and maybe even enjoy learning more.

And staff should greet and treat students to show they care about them. They need to be willing to focus on them and not their filing, or processes or paperwork. Nothing upsets anyone more than being shown he or she does not matter as much as making some marks on a page, filing something or talking on the phone. Concerned one will forget what he or she was going to write on a page, there are post-its for quick notes to be added to later. Filing, the same. And a phone call? If it is personal, get off the phone. If it is business, mention to the caller that you have to take a moment to tell another student you will be a moment or two helping another student on the phone. Then tell the new student. Both will accept that.

Leaders Need to Be Customer Service Advocates

Not all bad behavior is caused by students or staff. A disgruntled or grumpy administrator or faculty member is going to be certain he or she makes others irritable. A frown can be as contagious – perhaps even more so – as a smile. A rude administrator for example, can cause a happy, even polite, staff member (indeed an entire office) to react in kind. One manager who does not know how to provide good service to his staff is far more debilitating to customer service than any one student or staff member can be. The person at the top of the food chain can feed everyone a sour pill quite easily. So when you look to see how customer service is delivered at the school, start at the top.

The first person who has to deliver excellent service to everyone is the president. If he or she is not capable of making people feel as if they matter and are valued at the very least, that sets a tone that pervades the entire institution. If the leader is someone who does not take the time to get to know the people who make him or her successful, the message that sends out is that people are not important to the president. This sort of not-a-people-person leader usually projects a sense that results and good numbers are more important than people. That makes it acceptable for others to act in a manner that indicates individuals are not valued.

If the leadership does not practice customer service and just talks about it, that will also cause a strong disconnect from everyone else. The campus community will realize that customer service is merely another of the passing trends that hit colleges every so often. We all have lived through them. We all know that if a phrase such as *continuous improvement* or *value added* is not genuinely supported from the top – and supported by actions, rewards and even sanctions – not much will really happen.

I had been talking at a customer service workshop about some problems I had discovered during a mini-audit of the school. The people who had set up the program assured me that this was something they wanted done and that the *right* people would be there to hear the message. There would be senior administrators as well as their staffs in attendance. It was not until the break that I found out that the for the most part the senior administrators had found other things they had to do and had just sent their staffers. The result was that the people in the audience were sent the clear statement that, "Customer service is really not all that important and if it is, it is important for you. Not me."

During the break, a staffer sidled up to the podium area where I was reviewing some notes for the next part of the workshop. She whispered something to me to the tune of "I didn't give this to you," and she dropped a folded piece of paper on the podium then walked away as if she had never been there. Here is what the note said (*names changed to protect the guilty)*

> We can't even get the information needed to get our job done efficiently – ask about getting access to the school's information system. I appreciate your info, but it seems like you have the wrong audience! This group has no influence on some of your suggestions. I would suggest you talk to Moe, Larry and the administrators. Let's face it; we cannot change signage, class sections, or anything.
> Neal, I've worked at (the college) for more than 10 years – Moe (*the president)* has personally talked to me perhaps twice. There is simply no communication.

Customer service is going to have a very rough time taking root at this college. It seems the leadership does not really care, and it seems they prove it on a regular basis.

For example, as part of a mini-audit I attempted to register for classes in the term that would begin in the fall. I informed the person in the registrar's office that I took time off to register for classes. She almost blushed with embarrassment as she told me she would not be able to help me register yet.

She indicated that she did not have some of the information she needed to be able to better serve me as a potential student trying to make some decisions. I was told "I would like to be able to help, and I should be able to, but I am just not given that information." The issues ranged from what sections might be offered, to whether or not students were being accepted into a specific program prior to January. The program only began in January and would have a waiting list so I indicated that I would want to get on it early to have a chance to get in. She did not have access to the list. That was held by the department chair and he was only available in the daytime. And in the summer, he was often not in his office.

I asked if I could sign up for some of the courses to have a jump on possibly getting in to the program. I also asked if there were any pre-reqs. These are bits of information a student would need to have to decide on enrolling or not. The staffer had to say she did not know the schedule for the next term even though it was completed, had been sent to the printer, and was somewhere online in the College's computer system. She did not have access to the online information to be able to answer my question. She explained that she was not provided that information. She was clearly both quite frustrated and embarrassed. She wanted to do her job but was thwarted by a top-down system and attitude that simply let every employee further down the line know they were not as valuable or as important as the ones above them.

The result is the college has some very serious problems that will not be taken care of. Students will suffer and not get the education they want and should get. Moreover, the people who work at the college will not receive the service or the support they deserve and need either.

If the leadership of a college, university or school does not serve its constituents, the staff will not – or maybe cannot – serve students. It is as simple and as direct as that.

The Campus

Enrollment, Metaphors and Poetry

A customer service facet that is often overlooked is the ***objective correlative*** aspects of a college. The phrase *objective correlative* is one taken from my English background and was discussed primarily with literature, but I find it has numerous applications to colleges. Besides, using the phrase helps justify all those years of study.

The phrase was popularized by the American poet TS Elliot to explain emotional reactions to literature. Objective correlative refers to a physical object or more likely a grouping or combination of objects, images, or visual descriptions that create(s) an emotional response to a piece of literature. For example, if a poem has images of grey things, a tumbledown house and crows sitting on a broken fence, these physical objects could set a tone, an emotional metaphoric response, of gloom and foreboding. Try an Edgar Alan Poe poem for examples and pleasure.

In a college, the objective correlatives are physical aspects of the school – websites, the grounds, the buildings themselves, the colors we choose in the buildings, walkways, signs, offices, lobbies, etc. These all have a very powerful response on a potential student's emotional reaction to the school, and they do affect his or her decision to enroll and/or stay. These all create a visual metaphor of the school and its potential to meet the three returns on investment all students bring with them. The three ROI's – fiscal, emotional and affective – are what help determine if a student enrolls, and as explained earlier they will definitely be the determining factors in whether a student stays at a school, transfers or drops out.

Stephen J. Tracthenberg, recently retired president of George Washington University, helps explain the power of objective correlatives in the minds of students in a Commentary "What I Might Have Told My Successor" in the June 13, 2008 issue of the *Chronicle of Higher Education* when he wrote the following advice on page A37:

> When I started at the University, students would come to me with a litany of complaints about residence halls, other facilities, on and on. Immediately we set about visibly improving things. After five years, although all was still not perfect, I began to notice that the people coming to my office hours were saying things like. "I'm having a wonderful time here!" Of course there were still complaints, but I could see that we heard turned a corner. Over time our efforts had enhanced the pace in the minds of the students ....

His advice is not only valuable for a new president but for older ones who wish to remain as well as for everyone at a university who wishes to improve the perception of the institution and what they do there. Positive appreciation of the objective correlatives reflects well on what occurs inside the buildings as well as the visuals themselves. Remember that the visuals are metaphors for the students. They say a great deal about the institution itself and cue affective responses that in turn will add to or reduce the sense of ROI for students.

We are aware that one of the most important parts of the enrollment process is the tour. But what most people don't realize is that a student has started creating a visual metaphor of the school as soon as they make contact with the objective correlatives of that school. The tour is generally that which polishes the metaphor.

Metaphors are very powerful. They become emblematic of the institution and are very hard to shake loose or change. It is important to realize that students think not in words, but in pictures, in metaphors of their world as Gerald Altman discusses so very well in his excellent 2003 book integrating cognitive study and marketing titled *How Customers Think: Essential Insights into the Mind of the Market.* Students live in a visual environment which has them read and value objects emotionally. They trust these images much more powerfully than any words, which make the images the coin of our realm. They make amazingly quick and assertive metaphoric leaps of judgment and embed them deeply in their belief systems. We view the world intellectually in words and numbers that we want to make some logical sense. We wish to have rationality be the basis for decisions. They use visual objective correlatives and the metaphors they generate.

All of this generates an inherent conflict that can lead to problems.

Campuses Are Not Retreats

We may wish to think that the academic campus is somehow a retreat from the hustle and bustle, curse and worse of the commercial world outside the gates, walls, or parking lots that border our colleges. It is not. The popular image of the intellectual and meditative retreat of dedicated scholars and young people yearning to learn is just an opening scene in a bad movie from some distant fictional clichéd past.

The same concerns, attitudes and personalities that live off campus or in the dorms come into the halls and classrooms everyday. People who are unhappy off campus will be unhappy on campus. People who are rude in stores will be rude in offices. Those who are impatient waiting to get a seat in a restaurant will not be any more patient in any line on campus. Individuals who treat people poorly in a mall will not suddenly be nice in an office on campus. And nice people will try to stay nice unless we treat them in a malicious manner.

And of course we do just that first thing in the morning as they arrive on most campuses.

We greet our students and others with such welcoming and warm fuzzy prominent signs as FACULTY AND STAFF PARKING ONLY. VIOLATORS WILL BE TICKETED AND TOWED. There is no better way to make sure people can get into a bad mood than the way colleges assign parking permits and parking lots on campus. What a wonderful way to say "Hello and you are not important to us." At the mall, students can park anywhere and not even have to pay for the opportunity as they do at many schools. But at institutions of higher learning, they are second-class parkers who are often charged for the privilege.

A long frustrating hunt for an open parking spot, followed by a dash to class is sufficient enough to tell your student he or she is not as important as the faculty and administrators who get the parking lots close to their offices.

It should not surprise anyone that parking is consistently found to be one of the top five student (and employee) complaints in most every customer service survey conducted. The following is drawn from a customer service audit of a college with a retention problem that began with its approach to commuters and parking.

Losing Enrollment in Lot C

When doing an audit, AcademicMAPS studies every service and marketing aspect of a school. We act as would potential students and see what it feels like to attend the institution. So we do everything a student would do when coming on campus for the first time. Once we're *in* we check out, explore, and measure every aspect of the service at the place except one – teaching – the one area that is most important and central to customer service, but almost always it is not open for review. I wonder why schools would not want potential students to preview or try out a primary aspect of their purchase?

This particular college is primarily a commuting institution with very little public transportation access. So, almost everyone drives to come to the campus. We started out in our rental car to find the place. Turns out, that was a real chore. The directions on the website were not clear. They included the usual false assumption on the directions that, "Oh, you know the way. You'll find it." There was no indication of the correct exit off the highway or the name of the road that led to the college. Once on the actual drive to the school, there were no clear directional signs pointing the way once we did figure out what exit we should have taken.

Keep in mind that many students are quite tentative about college and are actually seeking reasons not to attend. The surest way to be sure a student doesn't come is to keep them from getting there. "Uhhh, Mom, I tried to go and register, but I couldn't find the place. I drove around and around and finally said the hell with it."

Try driving the route yourself as if you do not know where the school is. Just use signs along the way. Can you do it? Didn't think so. Just like the first time you tried to find your way for that job interview. Recall the anxiety? The angst? The distress? Potential students don't need any additional stress.

Make it easy for them to find their way to the school.

We did find the place, which was announced by a weather-beaten wooden sign and painted letters that had once been bright-white but were now faded and hard-to-read against the brown background. It was like a neglected drive-in movie sign from years ago.

We drove up the entry road and looked for posted signs telling us where visitors could park. We didn't find any. There were numerous signs like "A Lot – Faculty and Staff only – Sticker required – Tow Zone" and "B Lot – Faculty and Staff only – Sticker required – Tow Zone" and my favorite, "D Lot – Parking for Senior Administrators ONLY – Sticker required – Tow Zone". It appeared that the school was being overly considerate to its elderly administrators. This was particularly considerate since this small lot was right besides the main administration building where I supposed most of the senior administrators worked. Though there was not a noticeable wheel chair ramp for those who might need one. This building also was where the Welcome Center for potential students was located. Yet, there were very few reserved spots for visiting potential students and/or their parents. The parking spots that were set aside were also poorly marked making it even a bit more difficult to locate a space.

We finally did what many visiting students do at the college – we asked another student where we could park. We were told there was a student and visitor lot just a little ways down the road. Oddly enough, it was a huge lot that was rather filled up so it was hard to find a spot to park at 9:10 in the morning. There were six marked visitor spots but they were filled already by what I supposed were students just visiting a class or two since these cars had active parking stickers.

We then hiked in from Lot C, which oddly enough was the one

furthest away from the campus entrance. A, B, and D were closest to the buildings. I suppose Lot C was placed furthest away to encourage good health and exercise habits for the students. But then, why were the employee lots so close to the buildings? I would have thought they would be further out to encourage walking for health for those on the payroll. After all, mounting medical insurance costs might actually be lowered if they were healthier.

Physical health was not the issue. Political health was. The college's leadership did not want to take on the faculty and staff over parking. As we all know parking closest to the building is a God-given faculty and administrative right even if one is an atheist – or a student paying thousands of dollars for tuition and fees, and another thousand for books and supplies.

This upset me. Not that I had to walk, but that I had to walk because I might be a student.

Granted, in our society walking is considered work. Most people would be happiest if their office was a sort of garage so they could drive right up to their desk. That way they would never have their walking or running shoes touch the ground for more than a step or two. No one wants to have to walk distances. That includes students. But they are the customers and some consideration ought to be provided.

Appropriate customer service says the paying client should not have to be the one most inconvenienced. That includes having to park in the furthest lot out and then paying for the privilege of this parking discrimination. That creates unhappy and even angry clients who, as you know, ask "Why do I have to pay to park way the hell out there? I am paying thousands of dollars. I pay your salary after all (collectively anyhow)." Students should get to park closer to the campus.

Look at it this way. You go to a restaurant, or for that matter almost any store. You get there and drive around looking for a place to park close to the entrance. As you drive down the first row of cars, by the front of the place, you see signs in front of spots closest to the entrance. They say "No parking except for Head Chef – All others will be ticketed or towed." Others are reserved for the sous chefs, or the manager, maitre d', owner, daytime director, evening shift director, veggie buyer, meat buyer, etc. So you have to go to the next row where the signs say, "No parking except for head bartender, assistant head bartender, afternoon bar waiter, evening bar waiter, waiters, waitresses..." and so on. The next row is reserved for busboys and kitchen cleaning staff. So now you are circling around to row four and it is full of other patrons of the restaurant. Row five just happens to also lead by the exit from the parking lot and onto the road where there is another place just down the road.

Most people would be aggravated and angered enough that the workers get the best spots and that the patrons have to drive around looking for spots way to the back of the lot to leave. That tells you that the place cares more about its staff than about the paying guests. If you have trouble getting a parking spot and the place works harder to keep the staff happy than the clientele, will things get better once inside?

"There's that place just down the road, and I could do take.out for even greater convenience."

Unless the restaurant has something on the menu that no one else has or has the best something that you crave or is the only place in town, you are heading for the exit. What are this place's priorities? Not the paying customer.

As I and the team walked in across the hot asphalt, I wondered how many potential students had similar thoughts about this college and other schools like it, decided to head for the exit and purchase their education somewhere else. Our studies indicate 12 percent might be right. Twelve percent of, say, 300 students is 36 enrollments. At $10,000 annual tuition each, that's an annual loss $360,000.

Those 36 students will tell at least another six each that they had a bad experience. It becomes a geometric Malthusian progression.

The 12% is an extremely depressing loss particularly when the potential students had wanted to seriously consider attending the school and had made active moves to do just that.

Granted, not all students will not enroll or quit because of the frustration of parking issues. But one can be assured that starting the day with the aggravation of finding a parking spot then walking and even running to get to class on time will generate negative attitude.

Increase the Feeling and Reality of Security on Campus

The horrendous events at Virginia Tech, Northern Illinois, Louisiana Tech and elsewhere have led to a number of inquiries on campus safety and retention as colleges move forward to respond. There are no good answers for what happened. For the parents, families and the Virginia Tech community, there will just be questions and anger. I know unfortunately. Our family recently lost our 26-year-old son to bacterial meningitis. I deal with questions and anger over his death and thus know the emotions of the entire VTU community will be running very high for quite a while. I also know that when others know of my family's loss, they worry more about their own children. The tragedy at VTU will affect every parent with a student on any campus. They will look at their own children and your campus with a very protective and wary eye.

So how can we reduce some of the vehemence over safety and security services that will be suspect on every campus? How can colleges and universities work with an intensity that will be felt by every administrator and board member? Parents and the media are going to want to know how your school will make certain their child is safe on any campus. And keep in mind that articles like the *Wall Street Journal's* October 2006 piece "The FBI Stats Show Many Colleges Understate Campus Crime" will be likely kept in front of the media and public.

This is a time when a policy statement or reprinting brochures on campus safety on campus will not do. People will want action, visible signs that the school is taking steps to make the campus even more secure. If the campus is actually safe, great. Well done, But parents are going to want even more safety, assurance and visible actions.

Safety as a Metaphor

Visible is an important word here. What comes into play here is the concept of the *objective correlative*, which as explained earlier, works equally well to understand the effect of the physical aspects of a campus on students. The objective correlatives students and parents appreciate connotatively define the campus as a physical metaphor for the tone and atmosphere that defines a sense of security, safety and control. Since we all (and particularly our students) think metaphorically, buildings, grounds, bathrooms, interiors and all that is visible inside become metaphors – statements of meaning and values just as objects in a poem set the tone and add to perception of meaning.

Small things and small events can add up and generate the symbolism that figures into the appreciation of students and parents that safety, security and protection are in place.

So, and without cynicism, the appearances of safety are extremely important. The *Broken Window* approach that helped bring a greater sense of security and some argue real safety increases to NYC in the 1990's will help here too. The theory is developed in an article "Broken Windows" by James Q. Wilson and George L. Kelling in the March 1982 issue of *The Atlantic Monthly*. It goes something like this: If someone breaks a window in a building and the broken window is not repaired, people will assume that no one cares about the building. Therefore it is okay to break more windows because no one seems to care. So, more windows will be broken. Soon the building will have no windows. It is also likely doors will be busted in and more crime and havoc done to the building. But if the first window is fixed and re-fixed if needed, it is a statement that we do care and window breaking will not be accepted. The appearance becomes a reality in peoples' minds.

I was a skeptic of this approach at first when Police Chief Bill Bratton had the NYC police stop the homeless windshield washers from trying to earn a buck cleaning peoples' car windows at traffic lights enforcing public nuisance laws, public drinking, littering and so on. But it seems that the enforcement of these nuisance crimes created a metaphor for safety and enforcement for NYC. People believed the City and the NYPD cared. The feeling seemed to be, "If they were attentive to small nuisance crimes that made me feel uneasy, they must be really be doing a solid job on *real* crime." People and tourists began to feel safer. They were not afraid to be out in the City. Tourism increased as did the public's sense of security. And real crime did drop too. Although there are arguments as to whether or not the broken window theory and zero tolerance approaches were the factor, but NYC did become recognized nationally as one of the safest cities anywhere.

When I was Chancellor at a college, we employed a version of the broken window theory. We had a rash of books, I-pods, purses, computers and other personal items being stolen from students and staff. People were becoming uneasy about their safety in buildings as a result. They also assumed the administration was not doing anything to make them more secure. Word was going out to the community that the school was not a safe one. Enrollment and retention were being hurt.

We were working on it, but people didn't realize it or care. They just felt unsafe. We finally caught a book thief who gave us names of others he was working with. We called in the police to take them all out of the building in the lunch hour for maximum exposure. I also called a college meeting, cancelled classes so students could come and made some announcements on what we were doing to make sure they knew they were safe. We had hired three more security people for the building. We were changing all locks on doors and would be enforcing the locked door policy so when a room was empty, it must be locked shut. The college would randomly check college ID cards, and anyone without a card would be escorted off campus. We were moving forward to put in place a required parking sticker registration and any car without a displayed sticker would be towed. Light bulb wattage would be increased in parking lots and the number and wattage of perimeter lights was being increased as well. And the college would not tolerate inappropriate language or behavior in classrooms, halls, cafeteria, library, etc.

Faculty were asked to make sure attendance was taken, late students not admitted without prior notice, any student who left the class would not be allowed back in and would be marked absent, anyone sleeping in class was to be ejected, cell phones were to be off in class and if yours rang you would be asked to leave for the day and not come back in, computers were to be used for class purposes and not web surfing during class, and so on. And I personally assured faculty that I would support them in enforcing all this as long as classroom decorum was applied fairly, consistently, and without prejudice.

Within days, surveys, comments and interviews showed the campus was a different place. Students were thankful for our steps. They felt more secure and happier at the school. They were most pleased with classroom decorum enforcement since it changed the learning environment. Students felt inappropriate classroom behavior was cheating them. They were learning less as bad behavior interrupted class and the professor. One student summed it up well. "Now we see you do give a damn about us and our learning, and we care more about the school now too. I was outa here at the end of semester, but I'll stay now."

Ten Quick Security Steps to Increase Safety on Campus

Considering the various constituencies and politics on every campus, having the campus police/security enforce each and every rule will not necessarily work. For a few days, maybe even weeks, the community might accept greater enforcement, but that will end soon, though the admonitions of administration's oppression of academic or other campus freedoms will continue as a part of tradition. So what needs to be worked on is the objective correlatives that will be accepted and create a visible and real increased sense if security for students, parents and the community.

1. Have all employees learn how to say hello, smile and ask others how they are doing once they enter the greeting *zone*. As if they mean it. A faux greeting and smile is better than no smile. Also, teach them how to follow-up less than positive responses from others. This is important. The school must indicate it cares about each student to increase a collective sense of comfort through caring. This is also quite important for many reasons from identifying upset students to showing you care to learn what can be done to improve customer services and increase retention.

2. Stop petty theft on campus i.e. stolen books, Ipods, computers, purses, etc. This is for students and staff as well. There is apparently a great new product on the market to help on this

too. For example, a company named SafePlace rents and sells personal secure safes for students and staff to keep their personal stuff in whether they are in a dorm or set-up like lockers for commuters. They seem to be very effective too as stated in a letter from the Long Island University Director of Residence Life and Residences:

> *Student reports of lost/stolen personal property have been eliminated and reimbursement costs to the University have been eliminated as well…dealing with issues of lost/stolen property in the residence halls has been substantially eliminated…Parents have been fully supportive of this product to secure their students' belongings. SafePlace can also make financial arrangements that can even create revenue for schools while increasing safety. And don't overlook the value of these small safes in offices so staff can secure their personal belongings.*

3. Fix every broken light on campus and increase lighting in parking lots, pathways, halls and lobbies. Nothing generates a sense of fear more than dark areas. Yes, I am fully aware that lighting wattage has been lowered to save money. Calculate the cost of the lighting against revenue lost from drops who feel unsafe on campus. Consider also the size of your evening college and the revenue it generates that *is* lost when adults are nervous to park and walk.

4. Increase security patrols on foot and in cars. Park patrol cars not in service in the entrance areas to parking lots and other visible spots where they will increase the perception of surveillance. Make sure the halls are clean and uncluttered. Remove old posters, fliers and certainly anything torn or scribbled over.

5. Either wash off or paint over any graffiti particularly in bathrooms. There is graffiti resistant paint that can help out in this area.

6. Consider having all staff and students wearing college id's so it will be easy to determine if someone is not a member of the college community.

7. Do not ignore the safety needs and concerns of staff. They will be the ones to project a sense, a feeling as well as the metaphoric reality of safety and security on campus. If they are nervous or afraid their personal belongings may be stolen, they will surely project that to everyone around them.

8. Get out of the office, walk the campus and listen to students, staff and the community. Keep in mind that we have two ears but just one mouth for a reason. They will feel safer if you are out among them. Listening to them can also alleviate quite a bit of anxiety which often comes out of the feeling that the school does not care about them individually.

9. Send out email and fliers too. Let the community know you care and are doing things to increase an already safe campus. Communicate changes and improvements.

10. Have a campus safety and comfort audit conducted. There may be things that are problematic that you and other community members may not notice. This is the worn rug theory in action that is best explained through an example. When my wife and I were buying a house, we would often notice that the rugs were worn down or even worn out. But the seller's did not notice.

Why not?

We are animals of patterned, habitual behavior so they had walked the same paths in the house every day. Rugs wear out incrementally from constant foot traffic over the same area. But since it was incremental, a little every day, they did not notice the wear patterns that we could easily see. They overlooked the wear and missed what our external and objective eyes could see. After all, it had always looked the same to them. It might be worthwhile to bring in a new set of eyes to look for rug problems that you and others grow to just overlook because it developed over time and now looks like it was always like that.

Signs of Rites and Wrongs de Passage

A colleague who is a social scientist told me an interesting tale of how the *Hekowee*, a Native American tribe obtained its name. Their history can be very helpful for colleges that wish to enroll and retain students once they come on campus.

The tribe had decided that they needed to leave their ancestral territory, head northwest and find a new land where they could grow and prosper. They tried to follow the moon and signs from nature but realized they were hopelessly lost, at which time, the chief of the tribe climbed to the top of a cliff, looked over the valley below and declared with a scream of frustration, "Where the heck are we?" The tribe has been know by that name ever since.

Interestingly enough, many, too many, students and parents have invoked the name of that tribe as they try to find their way around most college campuses. Then after declaring their membership, they often either wander from place to place or find a student who may or may not know the location of the person or the office they are seeking.

Why is that? It is because we in higher education have a tradition of subjecting newcomers to our campuses, and now our websites, to a somewhat literal *rite de passage.* New students have to prove themselves to be college students at a particular institution by hunting down offices and people on campus and kill time and energy as they try to find their way from place to place with little or no help from the institution. After all, we had to go through the ritual of getting lost and confused when we first arrived. New comers should too. I learned how to get from the parking lot to the classroom after a few tries replete with aggravation and frustration. It was sort of a collegiate hazing, a test of my sincerity about attending the college. I found my way around without any helpful signs, so why shouldn't they?

The core of the issue is the lack of signs as well as their effectiveness, i.e. signs that actually guide people to the right locations and help people navigate a campus. Or for that matter, even find the school to begin with.

Just a couple of days ago I drove to a college to meet with it about providing it some help with its customer service and retention issues. I was impressed when I saw a sign for the college associated with an exit on the highway. After taking the exit, there was another traffic sign indicating the college was ahead at a right turn a mile ahead. Unfortunately just after about a mile, there was a series of right hand turns but no signs to indicate which street was the correct one. It was my job to then play a traffic version of the old game show Let's Make a Deal. Should I try turn 1, 2 or 3? I took turn 2 and found myself driving through a section of the city that would make prospective parents wonder if we would want our child to go to school in this down and out section of town? This is a good method to lose a possible enrollment that was driving over to make the decision.

The turn was road number 3 as it turned out. But I had already started to be concerned about the campus as a result of turn number 2. What was so maddening for me was that the problem caused by the incorrect turn into a less than desirable area of the city could have easily been avoided if the school had just put up another sign or two. As it was, I arrived at the campus with no time to spare because of the wrong turn, and I was of the belief that it was the institution's fault; not mine. It made me late.

First impressions are so very important. Make a good one by making it easy to find your campus. We must realize that most students are choosing from more than one college, so if your school makes them feel confused or frustrated before they even get there…

Then when potential students arrive at the campus, make it easy for them to find a parking space. They should be able to find numerous signs that guide them directly and easily to visitor parking. Potential students should be treated as potential students, i.e. guests. Just as my mother went all out to make sure the house looked spotless and the food was special when guests were coming, the college should put its best face on and at least let potential students and parents park without being forced to undergo higher education's version of *Survivor: Parking Lot C.*

Make certain that there are enough visitor parking spots at least by the building where the admissions office is. And have these spots patrolled to keep staff and faculty from parking in the visitor spots. Too often, employees realize that the visitor parking areas are available and not patrolled so they become attuned to taking them. And, if at all possible, do not put parking meters up in the visitor parking spaces near admissions. Few things will turn people away faster than not having quarters to pay for parking when they are coming to meet you and about to make a multi-thousand dollar commitment. It is simply good business to give up a dollar or two in quarters for a parking space and gain a student plus tuition. If it is necessary to pay for parking, send the potential student a token to take care of the change issue. If a potential student will need a time and date sensitive visitor card to hang on the rear view mirror or lay on the dashboard, send them out ahead of time whenever possible.

There should also be a clear, easily read campus map by every visitor parking area. Yet there are very few colleges or universities paying attention to visitor or student needs to place campus maps near where people park. This is part of the *let's see if they can find their way to the office and prove they are smart enough to go to our school* approach. Getting into a parking lot can be a chore. Getting out and to where one wants to go should not be. If they have made it out of the car, do not push them back into it and off campus. Help them find their way.

When designing the maps realize that although most people on campus may know that Helichrysum Hall is the home of the admissions office, no one else may know that. In fact, the odds that a visitor would know that information is indeed slim. People come to a campus knowing they wish to get to admissions, billing, records, deans, enrollment, registration and other such places. They are seeking to complete functions; to get something done. They see the college as a collection of functions; not a collection of building names.

Here is a set of directional signs on a college campus:

Can you tell where the admissions center is? How about where one would go to register for courses? Attend classes? See an advisor? One hint by the way. Notice that Adams Hall states that it is One Stop? Ahhh, could that be an indicator of where students can have all their needs taken care of? A one stop student services area? No. It is for adult learners taking non-credit courses.

And the arrows, do they help? Not sure whether Adams Hall is sort of to the southwest or northwest. Arrows go both ways. But even if they were clear, they would not guide a visitor to where he or she needed to go to see an admissions counselor, pay a bill or for that matter do anything other than ship and receive a package. Those functions are set out clearly but no others.

The following section of a photo was taken on an actual college campus. The portion of a campus map it shows is a good example of a functional listing of the locations on campus.

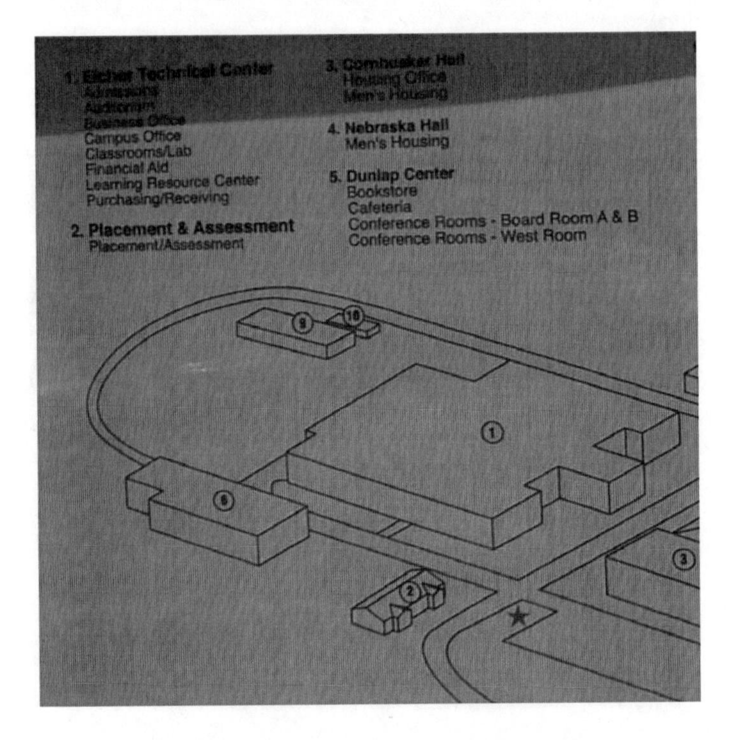

Note for example that under the Technical Center are listed admissions, auditorium, business office, campus offices, classrooms/labs, financial aid, learning resources center and purchasing/receiving. If a visitor were to come upon this sign, he or she could find the location sought based on the function he or she was there to perform. The only problem with this sign was that it was in an out of the way location in the back of a lot, but the college had the right idea. One worth considering and emulating.

Interior Signs Can Lead to the Exits

AcademicMAPS is hired by colleges, universities and career colleges to help them figure out why their enrollment was dropping. One recent client college was getting a large number of inquiries and leads but did not seem to convert them into applications then enrollments. The college was confounded, maybe even baffled, because students would call, set up appointments with the admissions and financial aid counselors and then not show up. Why?

Perhaps the admission recruiters were not really connecting with the students. Not increasing their desire to attend the school as much as they thought or believed was happening. Many times admission people will believe they have really pumped a student up when they are really just excited themselves over their own pitch. It has been found that students will often set an appointment and agree that they are pumped just to get off the phone from the admissions person. Too often academic salespeople (yes, that's what they really are) use a selling technique know as the *information dump*. They overwhelm the potential students with too much information. They seem to try to talk the students into enrolling by a never ending flow of details, anecdotes, and entreaties to apply. Potential enthusiasm drowns in a sea of one-way talk.

Or it may be that the admissions people do get the students to campus, but then they get lost enough to lose their enthusiasm and even leave the campus. This does happen 12% of the time by the way. Twelve percent of potential interested enrollments are lost when students make contact with the campus itself. Why? As discussed in the previous section, one cause is exterior signs but interior signs can be just as bad, perhaps even worse.

Perhaps photos from a few schools will help provide some answers.
Here is a hallway with a sign that makes sure students cannot easily find the admissions office. Not an office any college or school should want to hide from potential students.

There is often a simple answer to why students do not come to their appointments. They cannot find the office. We do not make it easy for them to find us. Look at the photo above as an example. The sign indicating where the admissions office is located is not just too small to be read easily, it is placed in competition with a larger sign that will draw the eye's attention. The larger sign is an excellent indicator of signage to make sure it helps no one who already does not know what is down the hall. Only people who work at the school, in this case a community college would know what is on the 200 Wing K250 to K265. The fact that further down the hall is a glass partition only helps to distract the eye away from the signs as well. Moreover, hallways themselves are always distracting by their open nature and the realization that one does not know what is further down the hall or coming up toward him or her. The mind is always trying to look ahead to see if there is any danger ahead and an overhead sign is not going to keep its attention long. The fact that this hall has two other hallways entering just at the point of the sign will also distract the eye and mind since each could hold something unknown and potentially dangerous.

Hallway signs all need to be clean, simple, eye-catching and immediately informative. They should provide information quickly and without any confusion if they are to be useful. They also should be accurate and up to date. Signs are of no value when they point out offices or people who have moved. The signs must also indicate the functions students must locate as was discussed earlier.

A College That Did It Well and Inexpensively

Below are some signs from Briarcliffe College, a career college on Long Island NY which did an admirable job when it installed signs to help students. The signs were designed to meet the criteria above and all-important cost factors as well. They were inexpensive to have made and placed, which also made them ideal when they needed to be replaced.

The following is an example of a hanging hall sign which I believe you will find much more informative and useful than the example above.

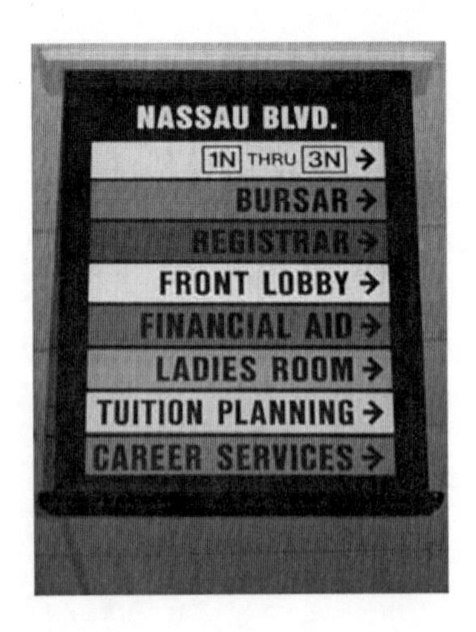

Each location and function area was given a separate color. This was done to create some contrast as well as an immediacy that would separate each destination. The colors were also continued onto the office locations as an added indicator that this is the right place.

Note that there are two hanging signs. Each sign was placed at any juncture that could lead to a student or visitor wondering where he is she is or where to turn next. The college built in an added redundancy to be certain that if someone progressed down the hall and other halls came into it there would be little chance for confusion.

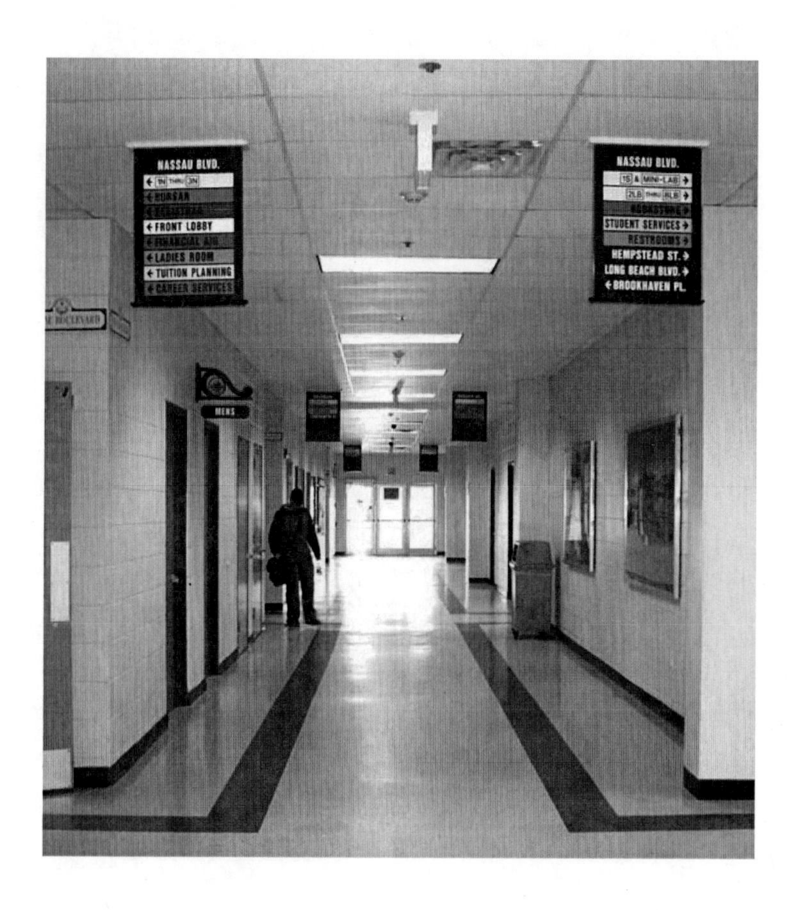

All hallways were also clearly tagged with at least one sign and usually a number of signs as well as the offices and rooms themselves. Redundancy can only help inform and reduce anxiety over not finding one's way. At all intersecting corners, the names of the halls were also clearly marked as well as every bathroom being clearly labeled on the door as well as a sign over the door that ran perpendicular to the door.

The signs (below) posted to the lest side of the door for each classroom were also made from Plexiglas and designed to allow notices and fliers to be slipped into them as an added way to communicate with students. These were very effective if for example, a class were cancelled or to notify students of any changes.

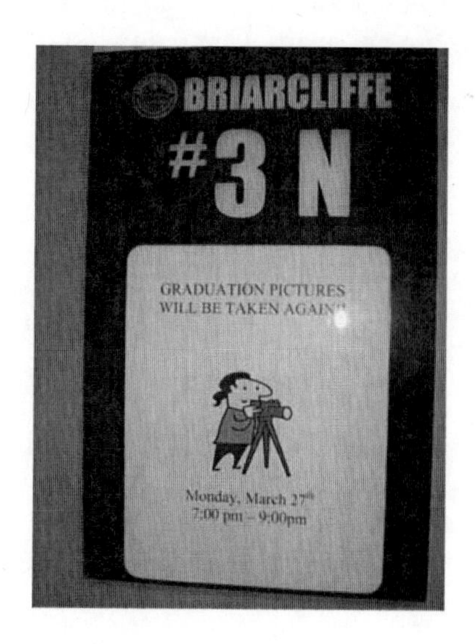

Briarcliffe did an excellent job with its hall and room signs. It became quite easy for students to find their way around the building. To make sure students would have additional reinforcement, campus plans were placed in every hallway as well as the lobby and the entrance area.

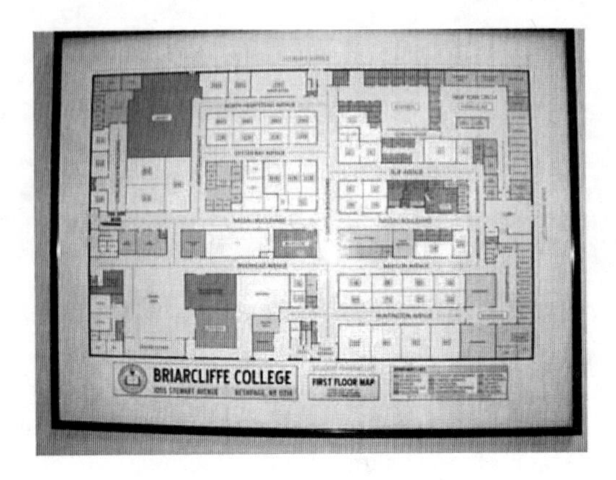

The campus map is color coded to match the directional signs. This reinforces the information making it even simpler for people to find their way to their location. And when a change occurred in the College, the signs and maps were redone to reflect that change.

How To's

Good Morning Captain

There was a time when college communities believed the campus was somehow a special place; a unique community of scholars and learners with a caring and refined core that made college somewhat idyllic. A mythical place that was sort of a slice of what I have been told is Midwestern communal spirit, though I must admit that I have found this so-called heartland goodness only on TV commercials selling bread or something not anywhere I lived. Yet, we did believe this was so. And if it were even close to a reality, that civility is woefully gone on most campuses.

Indeed many schools still refer to themselves as being a large family and maybe there is some truth to that. But then again, most families are rather dysfunctional so perhaps there is some truth in the college as family image. There are the familial rivalries as departments and programs vie against one another for positions, money and recognition from the parents – society and marketplace success. There is the usual Smothers Brothers family bickering of "Mom always liked you best and that's why you get…" And every family has it strange uncles and aunts who make us all blush from their antics, their socially unacceptable statements and behaviors. But hey what can one do? They are family after all.

But that does not explain a general breakdown in the social norms of behavior that I and others hear about and see both in academia and society. Customer service or simple service to one another has

declined it seems. It does not matter in this discussion why it broke down but there seems to be general acceptance that it has. And the work we have done on campuses does support recognition that if there were any service to our schools' clients, it has declined alongside of the deterioration in civility in culture and society. It has become a culture that Capt Kangaroo would never be able to fit in.
Captain Kangaroo?

Captain Kangaroo was the host of a TV show for kids that ran from 1955 to 1993. It was hosted by Bob Keeshan (the original Clarabell from the early TV classic Howdy Doody). Keeshan played a kind, easy going person who was never nonplussed by the antics of the characters around him such as Mr. Clock, Mr. Green Jeans and the tricksters Mr. Moose and Mr. Rabbit.

The Captain was the epitome of civility. He always said *please* and *thank you* and made a point of letting the viewers know that manners and especially the magic words were important. Moreover, an important section of the show came right in the beginning with a series of different people wishing the Captain "good morning" each day. The series of good morning greetings would always end with the Captain himself returning the greeting with his own warm "Good Morning" back to them before the show began. A simple but meaningful way to let the kids viewing know and learn what was a simple and common polite custom of our society. Other TV show hosts also greeted their audience such as Mr. Rogers who also stressed a quiet civility and ability to remain nonplussed by the pranks his assistances would play on him. He too stressed simple manners that were important folkways of our culture as did many other people. It was normal to greet one another even when just passing a stranger on the street or on the campus.

The simple hello was and is an important statement of recognition and value of another person. Yet, as I study institutions I do not observe the fundamental greetings that mark civility between people on campuses or communities. We simply do not greet or acknowledge one another. No hello, even sometimes when we know the person. Not even a nod of the head, a grunt or even better, a smile. It as if the other person did not exist or was not important enough to even be acknowledged as being there.

Actually, not recognizing another is a very powerful negative statement. It is an essential part of brainwashing. The process works to take away a person's sense of identity, of being. When one person does not recognize an individual's existence by simply responding to the individual's physical presence, the recipient of the behavior will feel deprived of his or her sense of value. The response to being ignored can be very strong, and the recipient will often do almost anything to be recognized as existing.

Try this experiment to prove this. Make an agreement with a group of friends or colleagues that when another person enters the group, you will all ignore the person. You will just act as if he or she is not there. Watch the reaction. You will soon see the frustration created and the power of ignoring someone.

The act of not saying hello to another as he or she passes you in a hall does not rise to the level of brainwashing or actively ignoring a friend, but it is a quiet, uncivil statement. It says to another that he or she is not worth my recognition. Granted, most of us no longer expect very many people to say hello to us as they pass us in a hall or on campus. This may well be a carryover from the urban folkway of not making eye contact with strangers so they won't rob you. But that just adds to the image of the campus as an uncivil, dangerous place.

If a campus is to rebuild its civility, it needs to reverse what is the poor customer service behavior of not greeting students and one another. In every other service business environment, a simple greeting is *de rigueur*. It is only on the college campus where we claim to wish to be enveloped and immersed in the higher values of learning and humanity that employees are allowed to be so rude as to not even pretend to be happy to see a client. Even the most arrogant, uncaring and supercilious medical doctor will go through the process of reading a patient's name to him or her and a mild pretense of caring. But in academia it is even possible for a faculty member to start a class without any opening or welcoming salutation to the students. A president or a more important administrator can walk a campus without ever greeting a student or faculty member. A clerical person or receptionist need not welcome a client before getting into the business at hand.

Capt. Kangaroo would be appalled by the almost total lack of simple manners like a please or a thank you. Even Mr. Rogers might get a bit steamed at the way we act toward other members of the community unless it were Eddie Murphy in Mr. Robinson's NeighborHOOD, whose uncivil ways might not even get noticed on many a campus.

It is important for retention that discourteous behavior be disallowed. It is important that people say hello to people and even pretend to be glad to see them. It should be a requirement of everyone who works at a college to have to greet one another and certainly say hello to students and campus visitors. If a college starts to do this, the action will increase the sense of value for one another and make the campus a more welcoming place – a place where people wish to be.

The simple act of greeting one another is a powerful statement of valuing the other being at the college and recognizing that value in a simple way. I recall a staff member whose whole week on a campus was made an enjoyment simply because the president said hello to her as she walked by in the hall.

Gordon Gee and the Tie That Binds

I used to wonder why Dr. Gordon Gee was worth over a million dollars a year to Vanderbilt, and why Ohio State University was so thrilled that he returned. It seemed to me (and actually still does) that no college president, EVEN ME (though I might be willing to consider it), is worth a million dollars a year; not even $900,000. It just seems excessive when others at the school are losing jobs to budget cuts and adjuncts are living in their cars. Are such high salaries really warranted or earned? Sure it is a tough job. But it is the same tough job at more or less money. Money does not make the job any easier, but it certainly does make some people feel as if they are worth all that money. As if they somehow are a campus treasure and should be treated as such. Others would do the job for less because they believe in the *calling*, president as a vocation. The others? Maybe college president as Louis XIV. We read about them in the *Chronicle* and online even at places like Oral Roberts University where one would think there would be a higher calling than excessive expenditures.

Why President Gordon Gee does the job and why he is so married to it, I am not aware, but the results are apparent. What he does is create community at the school and off campus too. He gets out and about the campus. He makes certain he is seen and contacted by students. He waves to students and others on campus and makes certain he is visible in the general community. And to be certain he is noticed, he has branded himself with a bow tie. He always wears a bow tie that he ties himself. And what's more, he lets everyone know about the bow ties.

That is an important part of the bow ties. Not that Dr. Gee wears them but that he makes sure everyone knows he wears them. That bow tie helps make him even more visible. When people see a bow tie-wearing man on the OSU campus, they almost always associate it with Gordon Gee. And when that man wearing the bow tie waves at you or smiles your way or says hello, you have been greeted by the President of the University. Even if it isn't him behind a bow tie, sometimes the effect can be the same. (He could even set up some kind of bow tie squad of Gee-look-alikes and have them walk around wearing bow ties and waving. People would think he is everywhere!)

"The President waved at ME. I **am** important."

"He's out there among us. We must be important."

Gee makes students, and others feel they are appreciated and noticed on campus by the president of the University. And if he cares, that must show that everyone else must also care. The whole university cares. And it is a very large one, too, one that can and must feel too large and impersonal for many students. But a wave from that guy with the bow tie can make it seem small, cozy and personal. Gee has a way similar to Bill Clinton that makes whoever he is with or smiling at feel as if they are important. And that is key to retention. Making students and all members of the campus community feel they are valued.

Get Out of Your Office

I am not saying you need to wear a bow tie. What I am saying is that to boost retention if you are a president, you need to be visible and known to students. Get out of the office and on campus. And what is true for the president is equally true for everyone else. Getting out of the office and saying hello to students should be a part of the job. Be out on campus, being seen, greeting students, saying hello and talking with the college community EVERY DAY AND EVERY WAY. Go to the cafeteria. Get a cup of coffee and join a group of students. Let them know who you are and simply ask them how it's going or some such broad "I care" question. Pass out your business cards. Imagine what the campus atmosphere would be like if everyone in the school spent part of his or her day saying hello, talking to students and getting to know them and them you. Gee has even been known to show up at fraternity parties and not lecture about the ills of drinking or partying even though he does not personally drink. He goes just to be with students where they live and have fun.

But the president of the school (and others) may say, "They'll call me, and I'm busy. I won't get my work done. Of course I care about students, but I have to show them that through my work and that means being in the office." Yet what must be considered is that not much is more important than retaining students. If one needs evidence just ask schools in trouble or for that matter review what your institution's second term/semester enrollment is projected to look like. Are the revenues going to hold? Is attrition higher than projected? Might some students been kept if they felt that the institution really cared about them from the president on up? Catch any irony here anyone?

Every college, university or career college that had its people out of the office whenever possible and getting known by students as people has increased retention and reduced student and staff problems, stress and complaints.

Make Every Day a Captain K or Bill Schaar Day

I had the pleasure and honor of working with a man who must have taught Captain Kangaroo. Bill Schaar was the dean of Student Service at Lansing Community College in Michigan, and he taught me an essential aspect of customer service. Dean Schaar would begin everyday by leaving his office. That might not sound as if it were a productive activity to initiate a working day, but it certainly was.

Dean Schaar would walk from his office across campus to the college cafeteria to meet with members of his staff and anyone else who wished to join the coffee klatch. On his walk he would greet every person he met with a very broad smile and hearty "Good morning young man or lady." He would then walk on. And the students all were left feeling recognized and appreciated by this man in a tie and suit who must be someone important or at least an administrator. This would be done even when he was not feeling in a very good morning mood. When he arrived at the cafeteria and the table(s) of colleagues who awaited him, they too would be regaled with an energetic "Good Morning my colleagues and friends. And how is everyone today?" He would do this no matter who was at the table including people I knew he thought were horses *patooties*.

Who he was greeting did not matter. The act of greeting did. He believed that everyone deserved to be recognized and given acknowledgment on the campus. Dean Schaar realized that every student and every person in the college community or on its campus was important. Students were why we were there. He believed that colleagues all must have a role and purpose or they would not be there even though he knew some could be removed without much of a loss. If someone was on that campus, they were going to be given the respect of a greeting.

Everyone should follow Dean Schaar's approach. Every individual on your campus is important enough for you to greet and ask how they are. I also suggest one more step. Grant them the extra value of asking how they are doing. And then listen to the answer. If the response is not one with *good, fine or great* in it, stop, turn to the person and ask why. Ask why the person did not say *good*, but also ask if there is anything you might be able to do to make it better. This is where a Customer Service Principle comes into play.

Just because someone else did a disservice or harm does not relieve you of correcting the injury.

If there is something you can do to make things better, do it. If not, take the students name and telephone number along with the issue. Tell the student you will see what if anything can be done and that you or another person will get back to him/her by phone. Get a good time and day to call back at the student's convenience. Then you must get back to the student at the designated time, even if it is to report bad news or no news. Once the commitment is made, fulfill it.

So smile, greet, ask and respond.

Students Hate Lines

As we do college customer service and retention audits, some common issues pop up for which there are some simple solutions. One problem found at most every school that has lines for anything is...well, lines. Students hate them and you should too.

Colleges lose as much as 3% of enrollment from students having to wait in lines. You don't like to stand in lines. I don't like to stand in lines. Students HATE to stand in lines, unless it is to be part of some major historical event, like tickets to the Super Bowl or the World Series. But paying a college tuition bill, registering for courses or dropping a course is not going to be viewed as worth standing in line. Colleges do not need to lose enrolled students to waiting in lines. In this case, we are talking physical lines as opposed to virtual lines caused by poorly designed web sites.

Here are a few customer service tips to help you retain students who could leave a line and never come back:

Appoint a customer service assurance person or two at the school. Provide these people both training and the authority to use that training. Place one or both of the service assurance people smack dab in the middle of any line. Have the person continually moving up and down the lines talking to students to assess your process, their progress and their level of frustration and/or readiness to bolt.

If the customer service assurance person notices a student who seems upset, the assurance person should go right up to him or her and try "Hi, I'm (name). Can I help you?" Next move the student away from the lines before the grumbling becomes viral. Let the student know that his/her place in line will be saved. "I want to help you and can do so better over here."

Go to a quiet place, away from others and hear him or her out. Normally the issue will be having to wait in line. Agree. Then ask what he or she is trying to get done. If you can solve the problem, do it. If you cannot, let the student know you will see what you can do to help out. Then walk the student back to the line. Say, "Thank you for letting me help you. I'll see what we can do to speed up the line," loud enough for others to hear. That's the message to get out.

By the way, if the student has an idea to get the line moving faster – try it.

Also have the assurance people act like an airline agent during busy travel periods. Review the paperwork students have with them to see if the documents are complete, the required information is there, and that they are in the correct line. Nothing angers people more than standing in the wrong long line!

An airline agent after talking with a traveler and ascertaining that the person is in the right area with the right paperwork may send that person to a digital kiosk to get a boarding pass and save time. In the same way, the customer service assurance person should see if a student can complete his/her business by computer or college kiosk.

Or consider letting students whose paperwork is in order step out of the line and drop the paperwork off to be processed later. Backroom clerical staff and administrators can enter the information or even wait until things quiet down and the lines end and later mail or email the student an acknowledgment that the paperwork is completed and entered. Also make sure that if there is a financial transaction, a receipt is sent.

"Yes. But what if the student is trying to register for courses and one of them is closed?"

Closed sections are a major source for walkouts by the way. But, when you provide the service of making the decision for them, odds go way up that you will keep them. Call them as soon as possible. Offer them another section. Provide him or her an alternative section thereby providing an alternative without making the student do extra work. If the proposed section won't work, continue with the student until you both agree on a replacement.

To make the time in line go by faster, turn it into a happier event. Hand out candy. Provide free coffee or soft drinks. Pipe in some music – Not MUZAK, but music students actually listen to. Make it feel more pleasant than the drudgery of lines.

And, DO NOT FORGET THE WORKERS! Keep thanking them. Encourage them. See if they'd like some coffee, a coke, juice, cookies, whatever. Make sure they know you appreciate them and their work. If they are happy and feel appreciated, odds are better they'll make students happier.

Techno-Eco Extremism – Cut Down All Phone Trees

I admit it. I am willing to be known as a techno-eco extremist. I hate trees. No not the green ones outside my window. They are just fine. Them I like. It is the technological trees. The telephone ones with trunks rooted in poor customer service. Trees with unfathomable branches of saccharin-voiced recorded messages that schools and companies use to keep people away from real people and real service. The trees I want to cut down are technological phone trees that are designed to do everything they can to make sure you cannot talk to a person, or obtain the information you seek, or solve a problem you called about.

I want to pull out my virtual chainsaw and cut down whole forests of phone trees that make certain callers obtain the very worst service ever available. It never gets the information he or she wants quickly and easily with any sense of caring for the caller. Phone trees and recorded messages can also make sure the caller slams down the phone with the gusto of frustration and anger. And as a result, they have major deleterious effects on customer service and enrollment. Potential students turn away from schools that can't hear or see the student from the trees.

Telephoning is the second most common method of contacting schools. The most common is the web. People are often directed by the web to call the school and talk to an admissions counselor. A practice that makes little sense for two reasons. First, the student is on the web and seeking to obtain particular information. If they have chosen to use the web, they have indicated a preference for it so why make them leave it? The answer from many schools is that they cannot supply the particular, personalized information the student is seeking. Their website is not capable of doing that. But with a simple web-based add-on such as Leadwise the institution can create an up-close and very personal website that can also become a powerful provider of detailed and personalized information requested by potential students.

The second reason given for directing students to the telephone is that it can allow more personalized contact. Students can speak to a real person. This works only if they can make it through the forest of telephonic horrors that defy allowing callers to get the warm, fuzzy of speaking to a person. The welcome of "Listen closely, our menu has changed" (as if anyone really cares about the menu) is not a very compassionate opening for creating empathy with a school. Unless the menu is on a quiz during orientation, do not mention it.

Students do not care about a school's menu. Their goal is obtaining particular information or a solution to a problem. So they have to listen to the long drawn out list of what numbers go to what possible extension. 'If you wish to talk with the bursar, press 4. If you wish to talk with the registrar, press 6. If you wish to talk to a person and tell them why you are calling because you don't know what that academic office you need is titled, press your stomach and make a wish, because we are trying to keep you from talking with an operator so we can save money while we lose you as a potential enrollment…

Students dislike answering systems and phone trees at least as much as you do. They despise holding on the phone trying to get to a person as much as you do. They want to talk with a real person a much as you do. They do not want to have to enter their student number in an attempt to gain assistance only to be connected to a person finally who starts the conversation with, "May I have your student number?" They enjoy that about as much as you dislike entering your number and being asked for it again and again.

They do not believe the phone message which tells them they can get their issue resolved by going to your web. They were probably just directed by the website to a phone number that is now telling them to go to the website. They know it is a continuous loop designed to make them go away and leave you alone.

They so loathe the statement that is heard when a caller finds a way to get to an operator. "We are experiencing unusually high volume, but your call is important to us and will be answered as soon as possible in the order it was received. Your wait time should not exceed 12 minutes..." If a call is important, it should not have to take twelve minutes to get to it. What the caller hears is, "Frankly, you and your call do not matter to us at all. If it did, we would hire enough people to answer the phones since we always experience high volume because actually we only have one person answering the phone." If the prospective student does wait on the phone, you can be certain he or she is on the web at the same time looking for another school.

The answer? Get rid of the automated phone system. Hire real people to answer the phone but make certain they are trained appropriately. This is what FACTS Tuition Management did after it tried a phone tree and found out that its client colleges were not happy. FACTS president David Byrnes realized he didn't like talking to a machine so why would anyone else want to do so. FACTS brought in some great receptionists whose abilities on the phone make every caller feel valued.

Columbus State Community College in Ohio solved any and all phone answering problems by setting up what is likely the very best call center of any college, and maybe any business too. All general calls go to the phone center to assure every caller is treated well and really helped. The people who answer the phones at CSCC are empowered to solve most any issue or problem from class schedule changes to paying bills by credit card to buying books and more. It's an excellent model that deserves replication.

It needs to be recognized, however, that just having a breathing person on the other end of the phone does not guarantee good customer service. They must know how to use it as an instrument of customer service. This is an art that is missing in the lives of many people. Having a person answer the phone with "State College. Yuh, what dya want?" or "Hold on for a minute please. I'm busy." doesn't help much.

It is important to train people on how to use the telephone. There are training programs out there that can teach most people how to answer a phone. If it is a business necessity to use telephonic technology, keep it simple and always provide a shortcut to a real person who knows the correct way to use a telephone.

Give a Name – Get a Name

One of the techniques worth knowing and practicing is called *Give a name – Get a name.* This is a technique that should be used in all customer service situations. It is especially useful when confronting an angry student or client.

Give a name – Get a name is just what is says. The service provider creates a community of two by entering into a communicative interaction by giving his or her first name to the student. The surname name can be given but only as reinforcement of the first name and after a pause, so the first name takes precedence and primacy in the listener's mind.

Last names are for business interactions or to place yourself into a power-based relationship with a student. The establishing of power through names can be seen in what we do in classrooms. "Refer to me as Mr. or Dr. Somebody while I demean you by using only your diminutive first name." Not that this is wrong as such since it is important that the professor-student relationship be established.

The student needs to at least initially accept the Orwellian relationship in which some animals (professors) are created at least a little bit more equal. In fact, in working with students we have found that they do not believe, "Hi. I'm Frank and will be teaching this course," as a statement of equality. They have come to the class to learn not be pals.

So, one way to accomplish Give a name – Get a name can be seen in the example that follows:

“Hi. I’m Neal.............. Neal Raisman. I’m the Vice President of Somethingorother.” (The first name is given than the title to let the student know what the person does. This helps clarify roles while also letting the student know if he or she is engaging the right person.)
Then the person asks for the student’s name.

“And you are….?”

If the student is angry he or she will often respond with “Pissed off.”

”Okay, Pissed. What can I try to help you solve?” The student’s first name is used to continue the building of a community between the two. Note that the response here is not to say you will help or promise more than can be done. That would be a sure way to simply postpone even greater frustration and anger for later if you cannot help. Not all issues can be solved or resolved as the student may wish so do not offer more than a promise to assist. The goal is to indicate a genuine interest in trying to help.

Once first names have been exchanged, a small, maybe tentative, (yet real) community of two is formed. If nothing else, it is much more difficult for an angry student to retain a full level of anger when you have exchanged first names. You are no longer just a nameless representative of the anonymous school. You are a person with a name – a first name. You could even be a friend when I have your first name. The exchange of first names is the initial step in creating a friendly relationship. Just picture a bar or social gathering where you wish to get to know someone. What do you do after checking your breath as you walk over to the person? “Hi, my name is…”

It is much harder to be angry with a real person with a name than an entity, a thing that has no feelings to hurt and no heart to break. So, giving and getting a name can defuse anger and allow you to provide better customer service, actually solve a problem and not get yelled at and insulted as the nameless representative of the school.

I knew that names are powerful and the technique worked with people but I found out from a faculty member at one of the ECPI branches that it also works with machines!

After a customer service and retention workshop for faculty and administrators in Virginia, Prof. Bob Loomis of EPCI College of Technology in Roanoke, VA provided a powerful example of the value of names. Prof. Loomis was responding to a discussion of the Give a Name – Get a Name technique we had just worked through.

It seems that he supplements his teaching income by doing some computer repair and consulting for businesses on the side. He will go to a business and do all he can to repair a computer or software issue right then and there. From what I can figure, he is rather successful at doing so.

There are however times when he has to take the computer back with him to make the repairs. In those situations, he provides solid service by leaving a computer behind so the customer has something to use. This loaner, he has named Freddie since it travels with him on all calls just in case, and he is with it a lot. Though Bob checks it each time to make sure it is fine, there are times when the loaner may develop a problem since it is used by many different people with different preferences and networks. He can be sure he will hear about it rather quickly.

One time Bob had mentioned to a client that he was going to leave "Freddie" behind as a loaner. The client was a bit confused until he realized that Freddie was a computer. Well, the next day Bob received a call from the client. "Freddy is having a bad day," he said. Not "the damn machine isn't working right." A kind, understanding "Freddie is having a bad day" instead.

The client was not dealing with a soulless machine after all but with Freddie (an anthropomorphized machine with a name and thus some human qualities.) Ever since that experience, Bob does not leave a loaner computer behind but lends the customer "Freddy". Complaints with Freddy have dropped, and Bob attributes it to giving people a machine with a human name.

It has been pointed out to me at times that Give a Name – Get a Name may not work with some people who act as if they are soulless machines and tools with personality deficits. There are some people that may have less friendliness and compassion than a computer. For working with people who have less personality and customer ability than Freddie, **Customer Service Principle 15** may be worth considering even if you know their name.

Not everyone is capable of providing good customer service.
That does not mean they may not have value somewhere.

That does not mean they do have value either, if for instance they are not capable of working pleasantly with students or are the point of tension in an office. It is important that they are placed away from interacting with your students and other campus clients, or your students and colleagues will develop names for them that are not very flattering, though possibly very indicative. When a person has a name like Quasimodo, The Thing or The %$#&#!, take that as a powerful statement of the person's ability to negatively affect customer service. Move them away from people.

Also, check the way the school advertises for new employees. It may be that you are creating some of your own problems by the way you hire. Be sure to include the need for a willingness to serve and help others as a job qualification. Being too mean to work at the DMV is not a job condition one should seek for those who provide customer service.

A Simple Solution to Phone Rudeness

I explained earlier how a college or university can lose as much as 12% of its potential enrollment when interested students make their first actual contact with the college. Schools lose students who are interested in attending when they take the steps required to make a positive decision to enroll.

This should not surprise anyone who ever heard about first impressions or has read the important book *Blink: The Power of Thinking Without Thinking* by Malcolm Gladwell. But when school administrators first learn of the 12% enrollment loss as soon as a student makes contact with the school, it comes as a surprise. Until they objectively look at their web or call in to an office on campus.

Not a week goes by without phone calls and emails from administrators who ask for help addressing issues and complaints they have been receiving from everyone from students to trustees. But a recently, an increasingly common theme has been complaints over phones being answered in a rude, indifferent, and offensive manner. It seems that people answering phones have been doing so while distracted, angry or apparently annoyed at having to answer the phone. These attitudes clearly affect tone and voice style.

There is something off-putting about a person answering the phone with an aggressive, "Yuh. What?" It does not greet the caller as if there is much interest in him or her. Nor does answering a call with the memorized canned schpiel that is spit out quite indifferently in a single breath as if it all were one word "NameofCollegeWhatCanIDoForYuh?"

These sorts of phone greetings tell a person he or she is unwanted or unwelcome, as if the caller is an interruption and an annoyance. If a student gets the feeling that he or she is not wanted from an early or first phone call, it can be an uphill battle to retain the student's interest in attending the school. That is quite unfortunate too since it can be so simple to assure that people answer the phone in a friendly and kindly manner that resonates with callers.

Here is one very quick and equally inexpensive customer service solution: Mirrors.

Yes. Mirrors. Go to a local craft store and buy simple, small mirrors and some double-sided tape. Give the mirror with the tape to everyone who might answer a phone. Have them tape the mirror to a spot level with their face or where they could easily see their face when they go to answer the phone. Then have everyone look into the mirror and smile before picking up a phone. All they need to do is retain the smile when saying "Hello, this is Neal. How may I help you?" (This is a version of Give a name – Get a name which can be followed up with "and with whom am I speaking?" once communication opens to complete the connection.) Problem solved.

It is a simple fact that when a person is smiling, he or she cannot answer the phone with an angry or negative tone. The smile will generate a more pleasant and happier tone. Even people with a less than pleasant disposition can sound welcoming if they are smiling while talking with another person. Moreover, the caller will hear the smile come through in the tone of voice. This may not eliminate all the phone protocol issues a school will have but it will certainly help.

Three Last Minute Solutions to Retain Students

Term and semester breaks as well as summer and long vacation periods are urgent times of year when attrition is one of the most important issues for an institution to be concerned with. Questions arise such as how many will drop out between now and the start of next session? The answer to this question will have major impact on the budget, purchases, hirings, firings and anything else that has budgetary implications – that is EVERYTHING. If more drop or step out than expected, then there is a tough period ahead.

Part of the solution to at least not exceeding the budgeted attrition rate is to provide students constantly good academic customer service. That is at the core of retention. But there are some potential solutions very well suited for the urgent times mentioned above. Here are three quick and effective solutions.

Final exam good luck card

One thing to do is for the president of the school to send a *good luck in final exams* card to every student just prior to exams. The period after finals is always a determining period when the student makes a go or no go decision to return or not. The stress of finals always takes a toll on students and especially the ones who might not be at the top of the Dean's List. During and especially following periods of stress, they consider if they are receiving the ROI's they desire and demand. They also ponder the top two hierarchy levels; Can I graduate and Can I get a job? A simple card signed by the president can do wonders in helping a student feel valued during this decision period.

The card in question should be an engraved card similar to what one might use for an invitation or a note card. The engraved name of the president on the front of a quality card may cost more than a computer generated one, but the effect is so much more authoritative and impressive. Besides, the cards surely cannot be more than the cost of a lost student and tuition.

The card needs to be mailed to the student personally. Send it right to the dorm room or home. The card mailed to the residence is a powerful way to show interest and concern. If the card is mailed to the home, it will also be seen by others in the home helping to make them into allies for staying in school.

We are talking a personal wish from the president and signed in real ink! None of this *Dear Occupant* or an open email to everyone. How personal is that? It will have an effect on them the way a Dear Occupant letter affects you. Remember the goal is to keep the student engaged in the school by showing an individual interest in him or her. To add to the strength of the card, provide a telephone number at which a student can call the president. There really will not be that many calls but the gesture makes a very powerful statement of concern. What calls do come are opportunities to help a student who may well have a problem, issue or be considering leaving for a reason the president can address and resolve.

The final exam cards can also be used for occasions like break, summer vacation, or any other reason. They are intended to make and continue contact with the students so they might be reinforced in their belief that the college is Cheers University – where the president knows my name and is glad I came.

Presidents serve the students

If you want to take an additional step, invite students to a free late night, say midnight, coffee and cookies/pastry/ice cream event the night before the first final exams. The president should be there to help hand out the coffee and food. Little says we like and care about you to students than free food handed to them by the president.

You may not get every student that night but the word will spread and you might get to them all over a period of nights. And do not be afraid to say, "Good luck. I am looking forward to welcoming you back next term." If a student does not respond with "Yuh.. See you then," that is a student who may be thinking or even planning to leave. This is the time for the president to ask if there is a problem. Listen to it. Try to solve the situation. At least get some response to that student ASAP.

Immediate help

If the student's issue is a problem of understanding or learning something in class, have tutors (preferably faculty not peer tutors) available that night who can help the student right then and there. After all, though poor grades are not the major reason why students leave a school, if they do fail courses, they may have to drop. Remember, giving easy or inflated grades is not customer service. Besides the college's larger goal is knowledge and skills through learning even on the night before finals.

This might not save every student who might be teetering, but students will find these positive statements will tilt back some students into the positive zone. And that can help revenue incline. into a more positive zone, too.

Greatest Gift of All – Saving Student Enrollment

Give a student, the school and yourself a present.

If you believe that students get a great education at your school – perhaps even better than that at another college – you should do all you can to keep students at your school. You don't wish them an inferior education do you?

To really give students a present, give the school the population it needs for next term. And to make yourself feel as if you really have accomplished something, start by getting a list of every student who has indicated he or she may be or is leaving. Call every one of them personally (but as if you do not know they are dropping out). A personal call is often all they need to change their mind.

Here's a script that works. Change it to your tastes.

> "Hi, (student name), this is (your name), (president, dean, professor) at (college name). I'm just calling to wish you a happy holiday and thank you for being a student at (college name). We exist for you students, so I look forward to seeing you next term/semester. Oh by the way, if I can help make your next term/semester better, just email me at (your e-mail address)_or call at (your phone number). Look forward to hearing from you and seeing you on campus."

Call everyone on the list and sit back. Wait for replies. You'll get some and every one you get is an opportunity to retain a student in the college where they will get the best education.

It is possible (but less effective and far tackier) to send a similar automated message to every student that is coming back. But for the potential, probable or actual drops, a personal call is needed.

If you feel that personally calling students is not for you or below your position, you need to ask yourself if you really do care about students or the school. It is suggested that you get over yourself and call. If you don't believe students get the best education at your school, you better be doing everything you can to change that. If you don't think it will happen, why in the heck are you staying there? If students and their education are not important enough for you to take the time to personally call them, you may very well be in the wrong job. Consider that it is likely you are not working at the college for the high pay and short hours.

Make Them Complain to Improve Customer Service

When college presidents or vice-presidents of student services, enrollment management or the such discuss having a customer service workshop at their college, university or school, they often wish to have it focus on the positive aspects of the school's customer service. This is understandable but not advisable. Part of the successful president's credo includes: *Always focus on the good. What we do well. Use that as a basis upon which to build.*

There is part of the problem right there. To improve retention through customer service, it is necessary to also and primarily focus on what is not done; on what is making students complain and leave. In fact, what colleges should do to improve retention is set up a system that encourages students to complain.

When told this, many presidents and other administrators are aghast. They are not sure they want to encourage their students to complain. They are concerned that will just encourage them to be unhappy and focus on the negatives. Besides, they feel, they already have enough problems and don't need more.

That is exactly the reason to elicit as many complaints as possible. It is very important to identify and obtain as many complaints as possible. A customer service and retention problem cannot be fixed until it is known about. If the college is not aware of issues, they sit there, fester, grow and then explode in attrition rates. So it is crucial the problems that cause students to leave the college be known as early and completely as they can be. Once they are captured, then the institution needs to check into how they can be resolved.

This is done not to see if the issues are valid prior to moving ahead to fix the issue. Every concern that students have needs to be reviewed openly and honestly. If it is only a problem for that student, it is still a problem. Keep in mind that if that student is unhappy or has a complaint, he or she may well get to the point of saying goodbye. That's how attrition rates rise. Individual students decide to leave.

If a student thinks it is a problem and may leave the school because of it, it is an issue worth exploring and fixing if it can be done with the answer of yes to the following three questions:

1) Is the solution legal and within rules and regulations?
2) Is the solution ethical?
3) Is the solution in the best interests of the student?

If these three can be answered yes, then fix the problem. If not, the students deserve an explanation of why it cannot be done.

Recognize also that it is true that if one student complains about something, it is likely others feel the same way and just haven't said anything. And at the very least, they have heard of the problem and will give it credence since it came from a fellow student. Complaint can multiply geometrically after all. One student tells six who tell six more who tell…The complainer tells another and another and the others tell yet others and so on. And so, individual complaints need to be dealt with. But first it is necessary to develop a way to flush out the complaints.

Most institutions make a half-hearted attempt to inquire of students as to what students are happy with and not pleased with. The tool normally is a student satisfaction survey developed by the VP of Students. Predictably enough the colleges generally do well on it so they believe there just aren't that many issues out there.

Surveys can be used as a starting point but they need to be developed by someone who does not have a vested interest in the answers. The student services group may be the best in the country but it is possible that they could have self-interest in the results. They could have, subconsciously of course, devised items, topics and issues that would lead to certain types of responses. Colleges need someone who is detached from the results; someone who is interested only in getting valid outcomes.
There are other ways to invite students to complain about those things that bother them. For example, gather complaints using comment cards like the Applegrams at Lansing (MI) Community College. These cards are spread throughout the campus and ask students and others to comment on the service they received. An apple a day idea at work here.

We have recommended to colleges that they create an email address just for complaints, or even better, a blog to discuss issues students have. The advantage of a blog for discussion of issues is that it is interactive and can allow for anonymity. In most every case it is better to have all comments signed. Some student posters will provide their names and some won't but if you can get a name, it is always better. First you set up a community. Second, names provide a level of integrity to the issue. And third, you have someone to get back to with a solution or a description of the review and resolution of the issue.

Anonymous postings will necessarily bring with them some suspicion of course, and there will be times that the hesitation to accept an anonymous posting at face value is present, but to open the discussion anonymity can help. It can also add a nasty tone to some postings, so a tough skin could be helpful. But when the purpose is to allow for open comments, it may be advisable to allow for anonymous postings. Just use them with caution and look for trends not a single statement.

It is extremely important if a school uses a specific email box or a blog to always and quickly acknowledge the comment or complaint. Emails or postings that sit there without notification of someone reading them will simply add to any belief that the college does not really care, and this is just a false show of concern. It is best to do so in a way that can let others know of it so they can join into the discussion. This of course is the advantage of a blog. Any posting can be added to the previous ones and available for all to read.

A wiki has added advantages since anyone who enters it can add to or change previous statements to make them clearer, add more information or even refute them. Wikis can also be more immediate and community building than blogs which do have a static level. In a wiki, a university can make a statement and allow everyone who comes to it to change it. This approach could be particularly valuable when posting a possible solution on a wiki and letting people add to or change it to make it better for them. This of course places a great deal of authority in the wisdom of the crowd, but it has often been found that the student body can have a better fix for its issues and problems than we might, so it could be worth the effort.

It might be thought that public postings would broadcast any problems and tell everyone the college has issues. As a result, many presidents can become concerned about "hanging out soiled linen in the public". They fear that public postings could just multiply the problems and hurt the institution's image. And that could happen if the issues are not respond to and if there is no attempt to resolve the problems. If the school accepts it's not yet perfect and let's students know what they already know, it will get honesty points. Then when it resolves the complaints and publicly lets everyone know it did, that makes the school a hero.

The research is clear that when a business, in this case a school, owns up to an issue and solves it to the customer's benefit, it will turn a complainer into a supporter. Maybe even an advocate. If the issues stay out there and fester, the college could create a group of insurgents dedicated to hurting the school by relaying their complaints to everyone they can reach thereby proving again the Malthusian negatives of expansion.

In any case, the bottom line here is that it is better to know of problems than to pretend they do not exist and let them push students to drop out.

The 15 Principles of Good *Academic* Customer Service

There are appropriate incantations against attrition. They are not prayers as such, but they have the full power of retention when acted upon. And every one of them can and will improve retention. These are the 15 Principles of Good *Academic* Customer Service. Many of them have already been discussed in the text. Others are powerfully self-evident. They have expanded and even changed since the list was published in my previous book. The latest alteration took place recently and for a very important reason.

Websites must be well-designed, easy to navigate, written for and focused on students and actually be informative

Though the older Principle 7 above remains a concern, there is evidence that web sites are being worked on to be more attuned to student attitudes and the graphic basis of websites to better serve students. More and more colleges and universities call to ask for help in redesigning their websites to meet Principle 7. The recognition of the importance of the web is a reality for most schools.

I also realized that there has not been a school, college or university that I have worked for or studied where the faculty, at least, did not feel their students were not quite good enough for them. Most every institution wants to know how to recruit *better* students.

Every school seems to be after *better students* (than what they have I suppose, though few can actually enunciate a clear definition of *better*). Even colleges and universities that are considered selective to highly selective say they want stronger students. No one seems to be satisfied with the level of their students' abilities, intellectual curiosity or aptitude. They all believe admissions needs to recruit better students. They seem to want students who can already write, do calculus, think and know subjects at the college level. Students who will love learning in all subjects just as they who want the better students did not.

But the reality is that most students will not fall into that already intellectually prepared group of better students. In fact, they are coming to college to get smart because they are not there yet. It is our job not to recognize their brilliance but to amplify and add to what they bring with them, so they can become more intelligent in general and even competent in other areas, so they can leave college and get a career/job.

Even the best universities have to offer developmental courses to some of their top students. Check out some of the introductory course curricula offered even in the major name brand universities. Giving a course other than a developmental name does not make it non-developmental. Poetry for Physics Majors anyone?

There is not a school in the country that does not have to at least supply tutors for some of their students so they can pass a course or two. And this has always been true. Not every student, brilliant or not, is good in all subjects. Maybe not even the fellow with the PhD in Molecular Biology at 15 whiz kids. It might even be a safe wager that even some of you reading this book struggled and asked for help in some area of study.

The admission people have not failed the college when they recruit a class for it to teach. The students they bring in are what they could sign up for the school. They come from high schools which may or may not have really prepared them well for future study. They may be nerds, artists, math whizzes, writers, jocks, generally intelligent, over achievers, under-performers, unmotivated, awkward, smooth, tall, short, fat, thin, excited or bored. The one thing they have in common is they have decided to trust you and your school to get them to their goals. They are putting their future in your classroom. They may not yet be bright but then your job is to help them get closer to intelligence and ability.

And just as someone helped make you into the brilliant member of the collegiate community you are, you have the same job for each and every student in your care. To elevate them so they can join whatever career and community they seek in life.

If they already knew and could do, they wouldn't need you or your university. If they were already their best, what would there be for you to do? But don't worry; our high school grads do need you and your college to become their best.

So, Principle 7 has changed to become

The goal is not necessarily to recruit the best students. It is to make the students you do recruit their best.

Following the 15 principles can lead to enrollment alchemy that is golden. Review the principles with your college. Have workshops to discuss and implement them and you'll see leaden frowns turn to the brilliance of golden happiness of enrollment/retention success.

Here they are:

1. **Every student wants to attend Cheers University and every employee wants to work there! Where everybody knows your name and they're awfully glad you came.**

2. **All members of the community must be given courteous, concerned and prompt attention to their needs and value.**

3. Students come before personal or college-focused goals. Students really are more important than you or I are.

4. Processes, rules and products should assure that students and learning are at the center of the institution. If not, rethink them.

5. Be honest in all communications. Do not patronize.

6. Students can never be an inconvenience.

7. The goal is not to recruit the very best students, but to make the students you recruit their very best.

8. Just because someone else did a disservice or harm does not relieve you of correcting the injury.

9. Students and employees all deserve an environment that is neat, bright, welcoming and safe.

10. Students are not really customers.
    They are professional clients.

11. The customer is not always right.
    That's why students come to college and prove it on tests.

12. Satisfaction is not enough and never the goal.

13. Do not cheapen the product and call it customer service. No cheap grades. No pandering.

14. To every problem there is more than one solution, and they may be external rather than within academia.

15. Not everyone is capable of providing good customer service. That does not mean they do not have value somewhere.

Some Concluding Thoughts

Good academic customer service is not automatically a panacea for every problem at a college, university or career college, but it is a necessity for many of them.

Nor is it something that can be simply addressed by having a workshop for everyone and believing that the institution has addressed its customer service issues. Granted, a workshop, training session or presentation can have benefits and be reflected in retention. For example, following a workshop at the University of Maine in Fort Kent, retention was reported to have increased 5% by UMFK Provost Dr. Rachel Albert. This was 2% more than the administration had hoped for and was achieved because the University took the ideas from the workshop and made them part of the culture. It believed in what was discussed and put it into effect. It did not simply print a brochure and believe it had done academic customer service.

Developing and using good academic customer service is a very important factor to increasing retention and morale. It will bring a sense of integrity and caring to an institution. The college mission can take on additional meaning when good academic customer service brings the student and learning to the forefront. This does not at all mean that research has to be somehow demoted to make room for focusing on undergraduate and graduate student leaning. Not at all. In fact, good academic customer service will increase student willingness to learn and engage in their studies, which means greater teaching pleasure and even additional time from having to help disengaged students make up their work.

Moreover, one of the extremely clear benefits of customer service on a campus is that it will increase retention. More students staying in school not only allows the university to better reach its mission goal, it also translates into more strongly meeting and even exceeding financial goals. Additional revenue means more funding available for better facilities, equipment, resources; even more release time and travel funds could be possible.

Those are material benefits that can accrue. But finally, and most importantly, students come to a college, university or career college to learn so they can graduate and obtain a job/career. That is really why higher education exists. That is why so many of us entered academia – to have a role in preparing the future generations of citizens who can contribute to not just their own lives but that of the society and culture.

People enter and stay in academia because of the possibility of making the world even better through developing and imparting knowledge to the people of the future. These are the students who enroll at the institution. They are the future and will be able to participate best if they stay in college and graduate. And it is customer service that is the key to that.